THE WORLD'S FINEST
PASTA AND GRAIN

THE WORLD'S FINEST
PASTA AND GRAIN

RECIPES BY ANNE MARSHALL

RECIPE PHOTOGRAPHY BY PHIL WYMANT

GENERAL EDITOR MARGARET OLDS

STEWART, TABORI & CHANG
NEW YORK

Copyright © 1996 by Random House (Australia) Pty Ltd

Text by Anne Marshall
Food photography by Phil Wymant and Travis Trewin
Edited by Margaret Olds and H.D.R. Campbell
Designed by Stan Lamond
Food styling by Ann Creber and Janet Lodge
Nutritional analysis by Carolyn Kelly
Copyedited by Kate Etherington, Heather Jackson,
Susan Page, Melanie Falick and Judith Sutton
Typeset by Suzannah Porter
Index by Diane Harriman
Scenic photographs from the Random House (Australia)
Photo Library

Published in 1996 and distributed in the U.S. by
Stewart, Tabori & Chang
a division of U.S. Media Holdings, Inc.
575 Broadway, New York, NY 10012

Distributed in Canada by General Publishing Ltd.
30 Lesmill Road, Don Mills, Ontario, Canada M3B 2T6

Library of Congress Cataloging-in-Publication Data

Marshall, Anne E.
       The world's finest pasta and grains / by Anne
    Marshall : photography by Phil Wymant ; general
    editor, Margaret Olds.
          p.   cm.
       Includes index.
       ISBN 1-55670-453-4 (hardcover : alk. paper)
       1. Cookery (Pasta) 2. Cookery (Cereals)
       3. Cookery, International. I. Title.
    TX809.M17M364 1996
    641.8'22—dc20   95-47932
                                            CIP

Contributors: Michael Campbell, Sarah Kolberg,
Copeland H. Marks, Nicole Routhier, Amla Sanghvi,
Dolores Simon, Joanne Weir.

Film separation: Pica Colour Separation
Overseas Pte Ltd, Singapore
Printed in Malaysia by Times Offset (M) Sdn Bhd

10 9 8 7 6 5 4 3 2 1

Page 1: *This historic church provides an imposing backdrop for
these colorful dancers in Puebla, Mexico.*
Pages 2–3: *A cool morning mist rises from the Banda Sea
around Bandanaira in the Moluccas, Indonesia.*
Page 4: *The popular island of Mykonos, Greece, is home to
many eating places including this enchanting Italian restaurant.*
Pages 6–7: *Waters in the paddy fields reflect this brilliant sunset
in Vietnam.*
Pages 8–9: *Harvesting upland rice in northern India.*

Contents

Introduction

GRAINS, the seeds of grasses, have been an important part of the human diet for several thousands of years. Noodles and pasta came later, well after wheat was first processed into flour. As far as we know, the Chinese began eating noodles about two thousand years ago; and pasta was being made by the Italians at least one thousand years ago.

Grains were collected from wild grasses by humans before they discovered the process of cultivation. They learned, probably by accident, that if some of the seeds were returned to the soil, more grasses would grow, producing more seeds to harvest and eat. The stalks were cut, then beaten with a stick to loosen the grains. The grains were then pounded with a primitive mortar and pestle to separate the chaff covering from the edible grain. The result was nutrition-packed seeds, dry enough to store to provide a good supply of food.

It is believed that the cultivation of grasses was first developed in the Middle East, where wild wheat and barley grew profusely in the warm Mediterranean climate. The knowledge of this cultivation spread east to India and China. Today we enjoy the versatility of the wheat grain as cracked wheat which is strongly featured in the cooking of Russia and Lebanon, ground semolina and couscous (the finest use of which is made in Morocco), as well as the flour in "our daily bread."

Grasses which could stand a harsher climate, such as oats, rye and buckwheat, were cultivated in northern and eastern Europe. Millet, which tolerates a hot dry climate, was cultivated in Africa and parts of Asia. Later, maize or corn, a native grass of the Americas, was cultivated in North and South America.

Opposite: Part of the medina (the ancient quarter) of the Moroccan city of Fez.

A Chinese girl enjoys a hot dish of noodles from a streetside food stall.

Paddyfields framed by palm trees: tropical greenery on an Indonesian island.

Rice was first cultivated about seven thousand years ago, in the hot humid parts of Asia. Knowledge of this crop spread west to Spain and Italy. Many varieties of rice are now readily available—brown, short-grain, long-grain, basmati, fragrant jasmine and Arborio varieties. The paellas of Spain and the risottos of Italy are as distinctive as the pilafs of India and the stir-fried rice dishes of Asia.

Wild rice, a native grass of the marshlands of North America and Canada, is the most recent grain to be cultivated. And now quinoa, a wild grass with a protein-rich seed, once grown by the Inca civilization of South America, is becoming more readily available as its cultivation spreads.

Italian-style pasta is made from durum wheat flour or semolina, whereas Asian-style noodles are usually made from wheat, rice or buckwheat flour, although cellophane noodles are made from the starch of mung beans. Sometimes eggs are included in these doughs. Pasta and noodles are available, fresh or dried, in many attractive shapes and textures. The evocative names of Italian pastas—*orecchiette*, little ears; *cappelletti*, little hats; or *conchiglie*, shells—are as memorable as the dishes in which they appear.

All of these grains, pastas and noodles are an extremely good source of dietary fiber, high in complex carbohydrates, and provide protein, B vitamins, and iron. Day by day, we are learning and acknowledging the importance of a high-fiber, low-fat diet to help avoid or control and combat diet-related diseases. Some of the recipes were quite high in fat in

Overlooking the Vatican Gardens, in the very heart of Rome.

Greek soldiers in traditional uniform perform ceremonial duties in the nation's capital, Athens.

their original form—these have been adapted to reduce the fat as far as is compatible with retaining the authentic flavors. The nutritional analysis for each recipe includes the amount for total fat as well as the different types—the saturated fat level is the most critical in health terms.

Once these grains, pastas and noodles would have formed the basis of the local people's diet in their own regional countries. Today, with modern technology improving cultivation, communication, and transportation, most of us can enjoy the fine grains and pastas in an "internationalized" cuisine. With the help and guidance of the recipes in this book, you can enjoy them in your own home!

Good cooking, healthy eating and happy living!

ANNE MARSHALL

Light Muesli

This delicious light muesli, made with a bounty of unadulterated cereals toasted in orange juice and honey, contains very little fat. Serve it as a filling breakfast or as a healthy snack mixed with low-fat yogurt or milk together with colorful, seasonal fruit.

MAKES 16 CUPS

2 cups (6½ oz/200 g) rolled oats
2 cups (6½ oz/200 g) rolled millet
2 cups (1 oz/30 g) puffed wheat
2 cups (1 oz/30 g) puffed rice
2 cups (1 oz/30 g) puffed corn
2 cups (4 oz/125 g) rice bran flakes, optional
1 cup (5½ oz/175 g) soy grits or crushed soybeans
½ cup (2¼ oz/70 g) sesame seeds
½ cup (1 oz/30 g) wheat germ
1 cup (12 oz/375 g) honey
1 cup (8 fl oz/250 ml) freshly squeezed orange juice
2 tablespoons vanilla extract (essence)
1 teaspoon ground cinnamon
1 cup (2¼ oz/70g) diced dried apple

PREPARATION   *10 minutes*
✦ Place the oats, millet, the puffed cereals, rice bran flakes, soy grits, sesame seeds and wheat germ in a large bowl. Mix well.
✦ Preheat the oven to 350°F (180°C).
✦ Line 2 baking sheets (trays) with aluminum foil.

COOKING   *40 minutes*
✦ Place the honey, orange juice, vanilla and cinnamon in a small, heavy-bottomed saucepan. Stir over low heat until the mixture is thin and evenly mixed. Cool slightly.
✦ Divide the cereal mixture between the baking sheets and spread out evenly. Pour the honey mixture over the cereal. Use a metal spoon and fork to mix the honey mixture throughout the cereal.

✦ Place the baking sheets in the oven for 15 minutes. Remove and stir the mixture well, making sure to stir it up from the bottom. Return to the oven and toast, stirring after every 5 minutes, until toasted to taste, up to 15 minutes.
✦ Cool the muesli on the baking sheets on wire racks; then sprinkle with the dried apple. Store in airtight jars or plastic containers.

PER CUP
303 calories/1270 kilojoules; 10 g protein; 7.3 g fat, 22% of calories (1.1 g saturated, 3.6% of calories; 2.6 g monounsaturated, 8.7%; 3.6 g polyunsaturated, 9.7%); 49 g carbohydrate; 5.6 g dietary fiber; 28 mg sodium; 2.3 mg iron; 0 mg cholesterol.

The impressive Chicago skyline looking out from the John Hancock Center.

Light Muesli

Blini with Scrambled Eggs and Red Peppers

BLINI S YATSA I KRASNIY PERETS

While wheat and rye are the revered cereals for bread-making in Russia, the famous *blini* are made from flour ground from buckwheat. The Russians serve these in various ways—the toppings can be sweet or savory.

SERVES 4

BATTER

½ oz (15 g) fresh yeast or ¼ oz
   (7 g) active dry yeast
¼ of a 50 mg vitamin C tablet,
   crushed
3 tablespoons lukewarm water
1 cup (4 oz/125 g) buckwheat
   flour
1 cup (5 oz/155 g) whole-wheat
   (wholemeal) flour
½ teaspoon salt
1½ cups (12 fl oz/360 ml)
   lukewarm skim milk
1 large egg, beaten
2 tablespoons melted butter

2 tablespoons (1 oz/30 g) butter
   plus extra if required
1 large red bell pepper (capsicum)
¼ teaspoon paprika
1 garlic clove, crushed
1 tablespoon chopped parsley
1 teaspoon white wine vinegar
6 large eggs
3 tablespoons light cream or milk
2 tablespoons snipped chives plus
   extra for garnish
generous pinch salt
generous pinch freshly ground
   white pepper

PREPARATION *15 minutes plus 30 minutes rising time*
◆ In a small bowl, dissolve the yeast and vitamin C in the lukewarm water.
◆ Sift the flours into a warm, large mixing bowl. Sprinkle the salt around the edge and make a hollow in the center.
◆ Pour the yeast mixture, ¼ cup of the lukewarm milk, beaten egg and melted butter into the center of the flour. Using a wooden spoon, stir the flour into the liquid, then beat with the back of the spoon to form a smooth batter.
◆ Cover the mixing bowl with plastic wrap, top with a thick towel, and leave in a warm place to rise for 30 minutes.
◆ Heat the remaining milk to boiling. Add to the batter and mix until combined. The batter is now ready for cooking.

COOKING   *45 minutes*
◆ Heat 2 teaspoons of the butter in a medium-sized, non-stick skillet over medium heat and swirl around to cover the base of the skillet.
◆ Using a tablespoon or large cooking spoon, drop spoonfuls of the batter from the point of the spoon into the skillet, to form small round pancakes. When small bubbles form on the surface, turn the pancakes over and cook on the other side until they are browned and puffed.
◆ Place the pancakes on a clean cloth on top of a wire cooling rack, cover with another cloth and keep warm. Continue to cook all the batter in the same manner, adding extra butter as required.

◆ Cut the bell pepper into segments, following the natural markings on the skin. Carefully remove the core and seeds.
◆ Heat the broiler (grill) and broil the pepper, skin side up, until the skin shrinks and is slightly scorched. Remove from the broiler, place in a plastic bag, seal, cover with a cloth and leave to stand for 5 minutes. Remove the pepper from the bag and carefully rub off the skin.
◆ Cut half of the pepper into thick strips and set aside. Place the remaining segments in a food processor or blender. Add the paprika, garlic, parsley and vinegar and blend to form a textured sauce.
◆ In a small mixing bowl and with a fork, beat the eggs with the cream, the 2 tablespoons of snipped chives, salt and pepper until the mixture runs smoothly through the tines of the fork.
◆ Melt 1 tablespoon of the butter in a small, heavy-bottomed saucepan over low heat. Pour in the egg mixture and cook over low-medium heat, stirring frequently with a wooden spoon, until the eggs are softly set with a spongy texture, but are not runny.
◆ To serve, place the pancakes on dinner plates, top with the scrambled egg and the bell pepper strips, and drizzle with a little bell pepper sauce. Garnish with the extra chives.

PER SERVING
480 calories/2011 kilojoules; 24 g protein; 23 g fat, 43% of calories (11 g saturated, 20.6% of calories; 7 g monounsaturated, 12.9%; 5 g polyunsaturated, 9.5%); 45 g carbohydrate; 9.1 g dietary fiber; 586 mg sodium; 4.2 mg iron; 350 mg cholesterol.

Watercress Soup with Chicken Meatballs
XI YANG CAI JI TANG

SERVES 6

8 oz (250 g) ground (minced)
    chicken
4½ oz (140 g) canned water
    chestnuts, drained and finely
    chopped
2 teaspoons finely chopped ginger
4 teaspoons reduced-sodium soy
    sauce
generous pinch five-spice powder
1 large egg, lightly beaten
10 cups (80 fl oz/2.5 l)
    reduced-sodium chicken stock,
    skimmed of fat
generous pinch freshly ground
    white pepper
1 teaspoon sesame oil
1 tablespoon Chinese rice wine
    or dry sherry
1 tablespoon chili sauce
3 cups watercress sprigs
1 oz (30 g) cellophane noodles
½ cup coarsely chopped chives

This clear, light soup may be served and enjoyed during all seasons. Serve it as part of a Chinese meal or as a first course followed by dishes from other cuisines. The chicken meatballs can be prepared in advance.

PREPARATION   *30 minutes*
◆ Place the chicken, water chestnuts, 1 teaspoon of the ginger, 1 teaspoon of the soy sauce, the five-spice powder and egg in a bowl and mix until evenly combined. With cold hands, form the mixture into about 24 tiny balls. Refrigerate until ready to cook.

COOKING   *15 minutes*
◆ Place 4 cups of the stock in a large saucepan, cover and bring to a boil. Add the chicken meatballs and cook over low heat for 3 minutes. Using a slotted spoon, transfer the meatballs to a plate. Cover with aluminum foil and keep hot. Reserve this cloudy stock for another use (a soup or casserole).

◆ Place the remaining stock in a large saucepan and bring to a boil. Add the remaining ginger and soy sauce, pepper, sesame oil, rice wine, chili sauce, watercress and noodles. Boil for 3 minutes. Add the chives.
◆ To serve, place 4 meatballs in each of 6 soup bowls. Ladle the hot soup over the meatballs and serve immediately.

PER SERVING
138 calories/576 kilojoules; 11 g protein; 3.4 g fat, 27% of calories (0.9 g saturated, 7.3% of calories; 1.6 g monounsaturated, 12.7%; 0.9 g polyunsaturated, 7%); 13 g carbohydrate; 2.4 g dietary fiber; 691 mg sodium; 1.5 mg iron; 59 mg cholesterol.

Long Soup
TANG MIEN

SERVES 8

8 oz (250 g) pork loin (fillet)
4 dried Chinese mushrooms
1 tablespoon vegetable oil
1 garlic clove, crushed
¼ small Chinese cabbage or
    1 small bunch bok choy,
    shredded
6 cups (48 fl oz/1.5 l) reduced-
    sodium chicken stock,
    skimmed of fat
½ teaspoon finely chopped ginger
1 tablespoon reduced-sodium
    soy sauce
generous pinch freshly ground
    white pepper
12 scallions (spring onions),
    thinly sliced diagonally
4 oz (125 g) fine egg noodles

This clear, light soup is flavored with pork, Chinese greens, ginger and soy sauce, and is ladled over noodles. In China clear soups are traditionally served to cleanse the palate. This one is quick and easy to make.

PREPARATION   *15 minutes*
◆ Place the pork in the freezer for 10 minutes, then cut into very fine strips with a sharp knife.
◆ Meanwhile, soak the mushrooms in boiling water for 10 minutes, then drain and slice thinly.

COOKING   *25 minutes*
◆ Heat the oil in a large saucepan over medium-high heat. Add the pork and garlic and cook, stirring continuously, until the pork is browned, about 3 minutes.
◆ Add the cabbage, reduce the heat to medium and cook, stirring continuously, until the cabbage softens, about 3 minutes.
◆ Add the stock, mushrooms, ginger, soy sauce, pepper and half the scallions. Cover and bring to a boil, reduce the heat to low and simmer for 10 minutes.

◆ Bring a medium-sized saucepan of water to a boil. Add the noodles and cook until tender, about 5 minutes. Drain well.
◆ To serve, divide the noodles among 8 soup bowls and ladle the hot soup over each portion. Sprinkle some of the remaining scallions over each bowl and serve immediately.

PER SERVING
113 calories/473 kilojoules; 10 g protein; 2.3 g fat, 21% of calories (0.4 g saturated, 3.4% of calories; 0.5 g monounsaturated, 4.6%; 1.4 g polyunsaturated, 13%); 12 g carbohydrate; 1.2 g dietary fiber; 308 mg sodium; 0.6 mg iron; 18 mg cholesterol.

Watercress Soup with Chicken Meatballs

Soba in Soup with Chicken

TORI NAMBAN

SERVES 4

*4½ cups (36 fl oz / 1.25 l) dashi
(see recipe below)*
12 cups (96 fl oz / 3 l) water
*8 oz (250 g) dried soba
(buckwheat noodles)*
*1 tablespoon reduced-sodium
soy sauce*
*1 tablespoon mirin (sweet rice
wine)*
*8 oz (250 g) boneless, skinless
chicken thighs (thigh fillets),
thinly sliced*
*½ cup coarsely chopped scallions
(spring onions)*
1 carrot, thinly sliced diagonally
4 large eggs, optional
*shichimi togarashi (Japanese
seven-spice powder), for
serving*

Buckwheat noodles, or *soba*, became a food staple in Japan in the fifteenth century, and the Japanese still enjoy them today at thousands of noodle restaurants around the country. Buckwheat is a good source of complex carbohydrates.

PREPARATION *45 minutes*

◆ Make the dashi in advance.
◆ Bring 8 cups of the water to a boil in a large saucepan. Add the noodles and stir to prevent sticking. Return to a boil, then reduce the heat to medium-high and cook until tender, about 4 minutes. Drain the noodles and rinse under hot running water to remove the excess starch. Set aside.

COOKING *15 minutes*

◆ Place the dashi in a large saucepan, then add the soy sauce and mirin. Cover and bring to a boil.
◆ Add the chicken, scallions and carrot, return to a boil and simmer until the chicken pieces are tender, about 5 minutes.
◆ Meanwhile, bring the remaining water to a boil.

◆ Poach the eggs, if using, and set aside.
◆ Dip the cooked noodles into the boiling water to heat through. Drain well.
◆ Divide the noodles among 4 noodle bowls. Ladle the soup over the noodles, dividing the ingredients evenly. Carefully place a poached egg on top of each portion, if using.
◆ Serve immediately, with a bowl of shichimi togarashi, for each diner to sprinkle on top to taste.

PER SERVING

372 calories / 1556 kilojoules; 24 g protein; 9.1 g fat, 24% of calories (3.9 g saturated, 10.3% of calories; 4.6 g monounsaturated, 12.1%; 0.6 g polyunsaturated, 1.6%); 41 g carbohydrate; 6.8 g dietary fiber; 460 mg sodium; 4.2 mg iron; 282 mg cholesterol.

Japanese Fish Stock

DASHI

MAKES 4½ CUPS (36 FL OZ/1.125 L)

*4½ cups (36 fl oz / 1.125 l)
cold water*
*4 in (10 cm) piece of dashi
kombu (dried kelp)*
*2 cups kezuribushi (dried
bonito flakes)*

This stock is basic to the true taste of Japanese soups. To save time, instant stock powders and liquid concentrates are available in Japanese stores, but, not surprisingly, none of them are as good as the homemade stock.

PREPARATION *15 minutes*

◆ Pour the water into a large saucepan. Add the kombu and soak for 15 minutes.

COOKING *10 minutes*

◆ Gradually bring the kombu and water to a boil over low-medium heat. As soon as the water comes to a boil, remove the kombu and discard.
◆ Add the kezuribushi and boil for 10 seconds only. Remove the pan from the heat and set aside until the kezuribushi sinks.

◆ Line a strainer with a clean piece of cheesecloth and strain the stock through the cloth.
◆ Store the dashi, covered, in the refrigerator until required. Use for soups and other savory dishes.

PER CUP

5 calories / 23 kilojoules; 0.5 g protein; 0 g fat; 0.5 g carbohydrate; 0.1 g dietary fiber; 257 mg sodium; 0.1 mg iron; 0 mg cholesterol.

New Year's Soup with Rice Cake
OZONI

SERVES 4

4½ cups (36 fl oz / 1.25 l) dashi
    (see page 16)
4 fresh Japanese black fungi
1 chicken breast fillet, about
    4 oz (125 g)
½ cup (4 fl oz / 125 ml) chicken
    stock, skimmed of fat
2 tablespoons sake (rice wine)
2 teaspoons reduced-sodium
    soy sauce
1 cup shredded spinach
4 mochi (Japanese rice cakes)
4 slices kamaboko (Japanese
    fish cake)
1 teaspoon lemon zest
1 teaspoon shredded pickled
    ginger
8 watercress sprigs

Each region of Japan has its own version of this soup. It is traditionally served for breakfast on New Year's Day. You will have to go to a Japanese food store for some of these ingredients. Check the refrigerator case for the Japanese fish cakes.

PREPARATION   *35 minutes*
◆ Make the dashi in advance.
◆ Trim the stalks from the fungi.

COOKING   *20 minutes*
◆ Place the chicken in a small saucepan. Add the chicken stock and sake, cover and poach over medium heat until tender, about 10 minutes. (Alternatively, microwave the chicken, stock and sake on High for 3 minutes, or until the chicken is tender.) Cut the chicken into thin bite-sized strips. Reserve the cooking liquid.
◆ Pour the dashi and soy sauce into a medium-sized saucepan and add the fungi. Cover and bring to a boil, then reduce the heat and simmer until the fungi are tender, about 5 minutes.
◆ Add the spinach, chicken and chicken cooking liquid and simmer for 2 minutes.

◆ Meanwhile, cook the mochi under a hot broiler (grill), turning occasionally, until they are puffed and golden brown, about 1 to 2 minutes.
◆ Place a mochi and a slice of kamaboko in each of 4 soup bowls. Stir the lemon zest and pickled ginger into the hot soup and ladle into the bowls, dividing the ingredients evenly.
◆ Top each bowl with 2 sprigs of watercress and serve immediately.

PER SERVING
359 calories / 1502 kilojoules; 27 g protein; 3 g fat, 8% of calories (0.3 g saturated, 0.8% of calories; 1.2 g monounsaturated, 3.2%; 1.5 g polyunsaturated, 4%); 49 g carbohydrate; 3.5 g dietary fiber; 4088 mg sodium; 2.9 mg iron; 16 mg cholesterol.

A rice field in Japan; to the Japanese, rice is the food of the gods and no meal is complete without it.

Crab and Rice Noodle Soup

BUN RIEU

Noodles are an essential ingredient of many Vietnamese soups. A good source of carbohydrate, they turn a simple soup into a satisfying meal for any time of day. Dried shrimp, fish sauce and shrimp paste are available from specialty Asian stores.

SERVES 4

STOCK

1 lb (500 g) skinless chicken drumsticks
1 lb (500 g) pork shoulder bones
8 cups (64 fl oz/2 l) water

¼ cup dried shrimp (prawns)
1 vine-ripened tomato
4 teaspoons vegetable oil
1 garlic clove, crushed
1 cup drained, canned crabmeat
½ teaspoon brown sugar
pinch black pepper
1 large egg, lightly beaten
4 teaspoons fish sauce
1 teaspoon shrimp (prawn) paste
4 oz (125 g) rice noodles (rice vermicelli)
⅓ cup mixed mint, basil and cilantro (coriander) leaves
⅓ cup shredded green Chinese cabbage
8 scallions (spring onions), sliced
cilantro (coriander) sprigs, for garnish

PREPARATION 1¼ hours

✦ To make the stock, place the chicken, pork bones and water in a stockpot. Cover and bring to a boil. Reduce the heat and skim off any surface fat. Simmer for 1 hour. Strain the stock into a large saucepan.
✦ Place the dried shrimp in a small bowl, add enough cold water to cover and soak for 15 minutes. Drain.
✦ Cut the tomato into 12 wedges.

COOKING 30 minutes

✦ Heat the oil in a wok over high heat. Add the garlic and stir-fry for 30 seconds. Add the soaked shrimp, the crabmeat, sugar and pepper. Stir-fry for 1 minute.
✦ Add the egg and stir until well combined, then tilt the wok to spread the mixture over the bottom of the wok. Cook over low heat until the omelet has set, about 1 minute. Slide the omelet onto a plate and cut into 8 wedges.

✦ Bring the stock to a boil over medium-high heat. Stir in the fish sauce and shrimp paste. Add the tomato and the omelet wedges. Cover and remove from the heat.
✦ Bring a large saucepan of water to a boil. Add the noodles and cook until just tender, about 2 minutes. Drain. Set aside.
✦ Bring the soup back to a boil.
✦ Divide the chopped herbs and Chinese cabbage among 4 soup bowls. Top with the noodles. Ladle the hot soup over the noodles, dividing the ingredients evenly. Sprinkle each bowl with the scallions and cilantro sprigs and serve immediately.

PER SERVING
405 calories/1697 kilojoules; 38 g protein; 15 g fat, 32% of calories (4.1 g saturated, 8.7% of calories; 5.5 g monounsaturated, 11.8%; 5.4 g polyunsaturated, 11.5%); 30 g carbohydrate; 1.2 g dietary fiber; 583 mg sodium; 3.8 mg iron; 223 mg cholesterol.

Rice Noodle Soup with Pork and Shrimp

HU TIEU

This Vietnamese soup is traditionally served with a selection of accompaniments such as purple basil sprigs, thinly sliced small red chilies, lime wedges and fish or soy sauce. Dried squid is available from specialty Asian stores.

SERVES 8

2 dried squid
2 lb (1 kg) pork bones, trimmed of excess fat
12 cups (96 fl oz/3 l) water
8 oz (250 g) pork loin (fillet)
8 oz (250 g) rice noodles (rice vermicelli)
8 stalks bok choy
⅓ cup finely sliced green beans
8 small raw shrimp (prawns), shelled and deveined
2 large eggs, hard-boiled and quartered
8 roasted candlenuts or cashew nuts
2 tablespoons coarsely chopped chives

PREPARATION 20 minutes

✦ Heat the broiler (grill) and broil the squid until lightly puffed. Rinse in cold water and set aside.

COOKING 2½ hours

✦ Place the squid, bones and water in a large stockpot, cover and bring to a boil. Reduce the heat and skim off any surface fat. Add the pork and simmer until tender, about 1 hour. Remove the pork and set aside.
✦ Simmer the stock for 1½ hours. Strain the stock and return it to a clean saucepan. Set aside.
✦ Meanwhile, bring a large saucepan of water to a boil. Add the noodles and cook until just tender, about 2 minutes. Remove the noodles, drain. Set aside.

✦ Add the bok choy and beans to the boiling water, cook for 1 minute, remove and drain. Add the shrimp and cook until just pink, about 3 minutes. Remove.
✦ Bring the stock back to a boil.
✦ Meanwhile, cut the cooked pork into 24 thin slices.
✦ Divide the noodles among 8 soup bowls. Top each with 3 slices of the pork, 1 shrimp, quarter of an egg, 1 candlenut, some bok choy, beans and chives. Ladle in the hot stock and serve immediately.

PER SERVING
326 calories/1365 kilojoules; 36 g protein; 5 g fat, 18% of calories (1 g saturated, 5% of calories; 3 g monounsaturated, 10%; 1 g polyunsaturated, 3%); 29 g carbohydrate; 3 g dietary fiber; 1078 mg sodium; 1 g iron; 141 mg cholesterol.

Hanoi Chicken Soup

PHO BO

1 chicken, about 3 lb (1.5 kg)
4 oz (125 g) ginger, cut into
    2 pieces
1 teaspoon white peppercorns
1 lb (500 g) rice noodles (rice
    vermicelli)
4 cups (32 fl oz/1 l) water
4 cups (32 fl oz/1 l) chicken
    stock, skimmed of fat
sliced onion, for serving
mint sprigs, for serving
cilantro (coriander) sprigs, for
    serving
sliced scallions (spring onions),
    for serving
mung bean sprouts, for serving
chopped small red chilies,
    for serving
lime wedges, for serving

This ginger-flavored soup is famous in Vietnam where it is valued as a tonic. *Pho* means "your own bowl": the diners choose their accompaniments from a selection of crisp fresh vegetables and fragrant herbs which they add to the hot soup.

PREPARATION   *15 minutes*

◆ Rinse the chicken and pat dry with paper towels. Remove the chicken skin.
◆ Heat the broiler (grill) and broil the ginger, turning frequently, until charred on all sides. Rinse under running water and rub to remove any loose skin.
◆ Peel and finely chop 1 piece of the ginger. Place in a bowl and set aside.

COOKING   *1¼ hours*

◆ Place the chicken, peppercorns and the large piece of ginger in a large stockpot. Add the water and chicken stock, cover and bring to a boil. Reduce the heat and skim off any surface fat. Simmer until the juices run clear when the chicken is tested with a skewer, about 1 hour. Transfer the chicken to a plate and leave to cool.

◆ Remove ½ cup (4 fl oz/125 ml) of the stock and pour over the finely chopped ginger. Let stand for at least 20 minutes to develop a good ginger flavor.
◆ Remove all the chicken meat from the bones, discard the skin and bones and shred the chicken meat.
◆ Strain the remaining chicken stock, skim off any surface fat and discard. Return the chicken stock to a clean, large saucepan and bring back to a boil.
◆ Meanwhile, bring a large saucepan of water to a boil. Add half the noodles and cook until just tender, about 2 minutes. Remove the noodles, drain well and set aside. Cook the remaining noodles in the same manner.
◆ Divide the chicken meat among 8 soup bowls, top with the noodles and add enough chicken stock to fill the bowls three-quarters full. Add 1 tablespoon of the ginger mixture to each bowl. Serve with the onion, mint sprigs, cilantro sprigs, scallions, mung bean sprouts, chilies and lime wedges, to be added to the soup according to taste.

PER SERVING
349 calories/1459 kilojoules; 24 g protein; 4 g fat, 11% of calories (1.5 g saturated, 4% of calories; 2 g monounsaturated, 5.5%; 0.5 g polyunsaturated, 1.5%); 52 g carbohydrate; 2 g dietary fiber; 612 mg sodium; 3 mg iron; 65 mg cholesterol.

Vietnamese chili pickers with the fruit of their labor.

Hanoi Chicken Soup

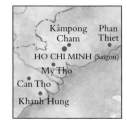

Chicken and Rice Noodle Soup

BUN THANG

This satisfying one-bowl meal is enjoyed for breakfast, lunch or dinner in Vietnam. It is garnished with cilantro to add fragrance and scallions to add texture, and is accompanied by tiny bowls of spicy sauces.

SERVES 8

1½ lb (750 g) skinless chicken drumsticks
1½ lb (750 g) pork shoulder bones
12 cups (96 fl oz/3 l) water
8 oz (250 g) rice noodles (rice vermicelli)
2 teaspoons vegetable oil
2 large eggs, lightly beaten
8 oz (250 g) chicken breast fillets
1 cup coarsely chopped Chinese cabbage
1 cup (2 oz/60 g) mung bean sprouts
¼ cup shredded purple basil
¼ cup shredded mint
1 tablespoon dried shrimp powder
8 scallions (spring onions), thinly sliced
cilantro (coriander) leaves, for garnish

PREPARATION   1¼ hours
✦ Place the chicken drumsticks, pork bones and water in a stockpot. Cover and bring to a boil. Reduce the heat and skim off the surface fat. Boil gently for 1 hour. Strain the stock into a large saucepan.

COOKING   20 minutes
✦ Heat the oil in a medium-sized, non-stick skillet over medium heat. Add the eggs and tilt the skillet to spread the mixture over the bottom of the skillet. Cook over low heat until the omelet has set, about 1 minute. Slide the omelet onto a plate and cut into thin strips.
✦ Bring the stock to a boil. Add the chicken fillets, reduce the heat and simmer until the meat is no longer pink, about 10 minutes.
✦ Meanwhile, bring a large saucepan of water to a boil. Add the noodles and simmer over low heat until tender, about 2 minutes. Drain, rinse well under cold running water and drain again.

✦ When the chicken is ready, remove with a slotted spoon and cut into long, thin strips.
✦ Add the Chinese cabbage to the hot stock and simmer for 1 minute. Using a slotted spoon, transfer to a plate.
✦ To serve, divide the bean sprouts, basil and mint among 8 soup bowls. Top with the noodles, chicken, Chinese cabbage and omelet strips and sprinkle with the dried shrimp powder. Ladle about 1½ cups of the hot chicken stock into each soup bowl. Sprinkle with the scallions and the cilantro leaves. Serve immediately with your favorite spicy sauce.

PER SERVING
184 calories/772 kilojoules; 11 g protein; 3.2 g fat, 16% of calories (0.9 g saturated, 4.5% of calories; 1.1 g monounsaturated, 5.4%; 1.2 g polyunsaturated, 6.1%); 26 g carbohydrate; 0.8 g dietary fiber; 522 mg sodium; 1.3 mg iron; 64 mg cholesterol.

Food stalls give passers-by the opportunity to sample the local cuisine.

Chicken and Rice Noodle Soup

Rice Soup with Shrimp
KHAO TOM GOONG

Thai cooks are famous for their deft ability to meld contrasting flavors. In this soup the fiery heat of chilies is matched with the pungency of garlic and galangal, the sharpness of limes and lemongrass and the fragrance of fresh cilantro.

SERVES 4

⅓ cup (2½ oz/75 g) jasmine or other long-grain rice
8 small raw shrimp (prawns)
4 cups (32 fl oz/1 l) fish or reduced-sodium chicken stock, skimmed of fat
2 garlic cloves, crushed
½ in (1 cm) slice of galangal or fresh ginger, cut into thin strips
2 stalks lemongrass, thinly sliced
2 small red chilies, thinly sliced
1 stalk celery, thinly sliced
4 scallions (spring onions), thinly sliced
1 tablespoon fish sauce
2 kaffir lime or lime leaves, shredded
2 tablespoons fresh lime juice
2 tablespoons chopped cilantro (coriander)

PREPARATION   *20 minutes*
◆ Bring a small saucepan of water to a boil. Add the rice and cook for 10 minutes. Drain and rinse well under cold, running water. Drain and set aside.
◆ Peel and devein the shrimp, reserving the shells. Cut the shrimp in half lengthwise.

COOKING   *15 minutes*
◆ Place the stock in a large saucepan. Add the shrimp shells, cover and bring to a boil. Strain the stock and return to the pan, discarding the shells.
◆ Add the garlic, galangal, lemongrass, chilies, celery, scallions, fish sauce and lime leaves to the stock. Cover and bring to a boil, then reduce the heat and simmer for 4 minutes.
◆ Stir in the rice and return to a boil.

◆ Stir in the shrimp and simmer gently just until the shrimp turn pink, about 3 minutes. Remove from the heat and stir in the lime juice.
◆ Ladle the hot soup into 4 soup bowls and serve sprinkled with the cilantro leaves.

PER SERVING
93 calories/388 kilojoules; 6 g protein; 1 g fat, 8% of calories (0.3 g saturated, 2.4% of calories; 0.3 g monounsaturated, 2.4%; 0.4 g polyunsaturated, 3.2%); 14 g carbohydrate; 1.5 g dietary fiber; 434 mg sodium; 0.6 mg iron; 30 mg cholesterol.

Noodle and Pork Soup
BA MEE NAM

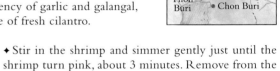

Soup may be served as part of any meal in Thailand. This light soup is popular at the beginning of the day as well as for a nourishing supper. Use the delicious, glazed, red Chinese barbecued pork if you can get it; if not, use roast pork.

SERVES 4

6½ oz (200 g) Chinese barbecued pork, loin or leg
4 cilantro (coriander) roots
6 cups (48 fl oz/1.5 l) reduced-sodium chicken stock, skimmed of fat
1 tablespoon finely chopped galangal or ginger
2 dried kaffir lime or lime leaves
4 oz (125 g) fresh egg noodles
1 tablespoon fish sauce
1 tablespoon palm or brown sugar
2 teaspoons peanut oil
4 garlic cloves, thinly sliced
2 lettuce leaves, thinly shredded
½ cup (1 oz/30 g) bean sprouts
2 small red chilies, thinly sliced
2 tablespoons chopped cilantro (coriander)
2 tablespoons chopped peanuts

PREPARATION   *8 minutes*
◆ Slice the pork thinly.
◆ Finely chop the cilantro roots.

COOKING   *15 minutes*
◆ Place the stock, galangal, cilantro roots and kaffir lime leaves into a large, heavy-bottomed saucepan. Cover and bring to a boil.
◆ Add the noodles, fish sauce, sugar and pork and simmer until the noodles are tender, about 5 minutes.
◆ Heat the oil in a small skillet over low heat. Add the garlic and sauté, stirring until golden, about 2 minutes.

◆ Add the garlic, lettuce and bean sprouts to the soup and stir well. Remove the kaffir lime leaves.
◆ Serve the soup in 4 soup bowls and sprinkle the chilies, cilantro and peanuts over each one.

PER SERVING
192 calories/804 kilojoules; 16 g protein; 5.8 g fat, 27% of calories (1.5 g saturated, 7% of calories; 2.6 g monounsaturated, 12.2%; 1.7 g polyunsaturated, 7.8%); 19 g carbohydrate; 1.9 g dietary fiber; 373 mg sodium; 1.2 mg iron; 35 mg cholesterol.

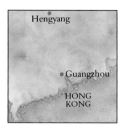

Spring Rolls
CHUEN JUEN

MAKES 12

Spring rolls come from Fukien, near Shanghai. The pancake-like wrappers are filled with shredded meat, fish and vegetables, then deep-fried to form a light, crisp roll. To make 12 spring rolls, prepare *one* of the filling recipes below.

PORK AND SHRIMP FILLING

1 tablespoon vegetable oil
4 oz (125 g) pork loin (fillet), cut into julienne strips
¼ cup finely chopped, canned water chestnuts
6 scallions (spring onions), thinly sliced
4 oz (125 g) shelled and deveined, cooked shrimp (prawns), finely chopped
1 tablespoon reduced-sodium soy sauce

CHICKEN FILLING

1 chicken breast fillet (about 4 oz / 125 g), cut into julienne strips
1 teaspoon cornstarch (cornflour)
1 tablespoon reduced-sodium soy sauce
1 tablespoon vegetable oil
¼ cup finely chopped, canned bamboo shoots
3 scallions (spring onions), thinly sliced
½ cup grated carrot
1 cup (2 oz / 60 g) bean sprouts

12 spring roll wrappers
1 large egg, beaten
vegetable oil, for deep-frying
chili sauce, for serving
mustard, for serving
plum sauce, for serving

PREPARATION   *45 minutes*
◆ Prepare one of the fillings.
◆ *Pork and Shrimp Filling*: Heat the oil in a small, non-stick skillet over medium heat. Add the pork and cook, stirring frequently, for 5 minutes. Add the water chestnuts and scallions and cook, stirring, for 2 minutes. Remove from the heat. Stir in the shrimp and soy sauce and set aside to cool.
◆ *Chicken Filling*: Mix the chicken with the cornstarch and soy sauce in a medium-sized bowl. Cover and leave to marinate in the refrigerator for 10 minutes. Heat the oil in a small, non-stick skillet over low heat. Add the chicken mixture and cook, stirring continuously, for 3 minutes. Add the bamboo shoots, scallions, carrot and bean sprouts. Cook, stirring frequently, for 2 minutes. Remove from the heat and set aside to cool.

COOKING   *20 minutes*
◆ Divide the filling into 12 equal portions. Place 1 portion of the filling in a line along the lower half of a spring roll wrapper.
◆ Brush the edge of the upper half of the wrapper with the beaten egg. Fold the bottom of the wrapper over the filling, then fold the sides in, and roll up tightly to the top to form a neat roll shape. Secure with wooden toothpicks if necessary.
◆ Repeat with the remaining wrappers and filling.
◆ Half-fill a deep-fryer (or a large saucepan) with oil and heat to 375°F (190°C). Using a frying basket or a slotted spoon, carefully lower 3 spring rolls into the hot oil and cook until crisp and golden, about 2 minutes. Drain well on paper towels. Continue frying as directed until all of the rolls are cooked.
◆ Serve the spring rolls immediately, accompanied by bowls of chili sauce, mustard and plum sauce for dipping.

PORK AND SHRIMP FILLING PER SPRING ROLL

90 calories / 377 kilojoules; 6.5 g protein; 2.5 g fat, 13.5% of calories (0.4 g saturated, 2.2% of calories; 0.7 g monounsaturated, 3.5%; 1.4 g polyunsaturated, 7.9%); 10 g carbohydrate; 1 g dietary fiber; 220 mg sodium; 0.6 mg iron; 40 mg cholesterol.

CHICKEN FILLING PER SPRING ROLL

81 calories / 340 kilojoules; 4.5 g protein; 2.3 g fat, 14.5% of calories (0.4 g saturated, 2.3% of calories; 0.6 g monounsaturated, 3.3%; 1.4 g polyunsaturated, 8.5%); 9.5 g carbohydrate; 1.2 g dietary fiber; 188.5 mg sodium; 0.5 mg iron; 20 mg cholesterol.

Villagers bringing their produce to market in central China.

Spring Rolls

Stuffed Tomatoes

TOMATES YEMISTES

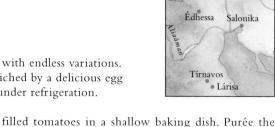

SERVES 6

*²⁄₃ cup (about 4¹⁄₂ oz/140 g)
    short-grain rice*
6 large, vine-ripened tomatoes
2 tablespoons virgin olive oil
1 large onion, chopped
2 garlic cloves, crushed
¹⁄₄ cup (1 oz/30 g) pine nuts
*¹⁄₄ cup (1¹⁄₄ oz/40 g) currants or
    golden raisins (sultanas)*
2 tablespoons chopped parsley
1 tablespoon chopped oregano
2 tablespoons dry white wine
herb sprigs, for garnish

SAUCE

1 large egg
*³⁄₄ cup (6 oz/185 g) low-fat
    plain yogurt*
*¹⁄₂ cup (about 2 oz/50 g) feta
    cheese, crumbled*

Yemistes or "filled vegetables" are a popular Greek dish, with endless variations. This recipe is an appealing light version of *yemistes,* enriched by a delicious egg and yogurt sauce. Only use eggs that have been stored under refrigeration.

PREPARATION   *30 minutes*

◆ Bring a medium-sized saucepan of salted water to a boil. Add the rice and cook until tender, about 10 minutes. Drain, rinse and set aside to cool.
◆ Preheat the oven to 350°F (180°C).
◆ Cut a slice off the end of each tomato, opposite the stalk end and reserve. Scoop out the pulp and reserve.

COOKING   *40 minutes*

◆ Heat the oil in a medium-sized, heavy-bottomed saucepan over low heat. Add the onion and garlic and cook until soft, about 3 minutes. Add the pine nuts and currants and cook, stirring frequently, for 2 minutes, then transfer the mixture to a bowl.
◆ Add the rice, parsley, oregano and half the reserved tomato pulp to the onion mixture. Mix well.
◆ Spoon the mixture into the tomato shells. Place the

filled tomatoes in a shallow baking dish. Purée the remaining tomato pulp in a food processor or blender and pour it around the tomatoes. Drizzle the wine over the tomatoes and place a reserved slice on top of each.
◆ Bake for 20 minutes.
◆ To make the sauce, beat the egg, add the yogurt and mix well. Add the cheese and stir gently to mix. Spoon the sauce over the tomatoes and bake until they are soft when tested with a skewer, about 5 minutes.
◆ Serve hot, garnished with the herb sprigs.

PER SERVING
*257 calories/1076 kilojoules; 9 g protein; 11 g fat, 40% of calories
(2.6 g saturated, 9.6 of calories; 5.6 g monounsaturated, 20.4%;
2.8 g polyunsaturated, 10%); 28 g carbohydrate; 3.3 g dietary
fiber; 149 mg sodium; 1.3 mg iron; 36 mg cholesterol.*

Stuffed Grape Leaves

DOLMATHES

MAKES ABOUT 48

*8 oz (250 g) fresh or preserved
    grape (vine) leaves*
*2 cups (16 fl oz/500 ml) beef
    stock, plus extra if required*
*¹⁄₃ cup (3 fl oz/90 g) virgin
    olive oil*
1 lemon, sliced, for garnish

FILLING

1 vine-ripened tomato
1 tablespoon vegetable oil
1 large onion, finely chopped
*1¹⁄₂ lb (750 g) ground (minced)
    lamb*
*¹⁄₃ cup (about 2¹⁄₂ oz/75 g)
    short-grain rice*
¹⁄₄ cup chopped parsley
2 teaspoons chopped dill or fennel
salt, to taste
*freshly ground black pepper,
    to taste*

No garden in Greece—no matter how small—is complete without a grapevine to provide leaves for *dolmathes. Dolmathes* are one of the classic *mezethakia,* the savory snacks that are served with drinks before the late evening meal.

PREPARATION   *15 minutes*

◆ If using fresh grape leaves, plunge them into boiling water for 1 minute to soften them. If using canned leaves, rinse them well.
◆ Place the tomatoes in a bowl, cover with boiling water and let stand until the skin splits, about 10 minutes. Remove from the water, peel and chop coarsely.

COOKING   *1¹⁄₂ hours*

◆ Place all the filling ingredients in a large bowl and combine well.
◆ Lie a grape leaf on a work surface and then place a heaping teaspoon of the meat mixture along the stem edge of the leaf. Fold over the bottom, then fold in the sides and roll up to form a small package. Continue until all the filling has been used.

◆ Line the bottom of a large saucepan with a few of the remaining grape leaves to prevent the dolmathes from sticking. Arrange the dolmathes in the saucepan, seam side down, in neat layers.
◆ Add the stock and olive oil and bring to a boil over medium heat. Reduce the heat and simmer gently, covered, until the leaves are very tender, about 1 hour. Add more stock if the dolmathes begin to dry out.
◆ Serve hot or cold, garnished with the lemon slices.

PER STUFFED GRAPE LEAF
*43 calories/181 kilojoules; 4 g protein; 2.4 g fat, 52% of calories
(0.6 g saturated, 13% of calories; 1.4 g monounsaturated, 30%;
0.4 g polyunsaturated, 9%); 1 g carbohydrate; 0.2 g dietary fiber;
48 mg sodium; 0.4 mg iron; 10 mg cholesterol.*

Stuffed Grape Leaves (left) and Stuffed Tomatoes

Risotto with Fennel and Asparagus
RISOTTO CON I FINOCCHI E ASPARAGI

SERVES 4

*8–10 asparagus spears,
    about 8 oz (250 g)*
2 tablespoons (1 oz/30 g) butter
2 teaspoons virgin olive oil
1 onion, finely chopped
*1 large fennel bulb, about 1 lb
    (500 g), thinly sliced
    crosswise*
*1 cup (8 fl oz/250 ml) dry
    white wine*
*2 cups (16 fl oz/500 ml)
    vegetable stock*
*1¼ cups (8½ oz/275 g) Arborio
    rice*
*¼ cup (1 oz/30 g) freshly grated
    Parmesan cheese*
*¼ cup (1 oz/30 g) toasted pine
    nuts*
*fresh thin shavings of Parmesan
    cheese, for garnish*

Rice dominates the Venetians' appetizer course and is often combined with such ingredients as sausages, lamb, chicken livers and even beans and raisins. This delicious, light spring risotto from Venice features fennel and asparagus.

PREPARATION   *10 minutes*
✦ Trim the asparagus and cut into 1 in (2 cm) lengths. Separate the asparagus tips from the stems.

COOKING   *40 minutes*
✦ Heat the butter and oil in a large, heavy-bottomed saucepan over medium heat. Add the onion and cook, stirring, for 1 minute. Add the fennel, reduce the heat to low, cover and cook, occasionally shaking the pan from side to side while it is still in contact with the heat, for 5 minutes.
✦ Add the wine, increase the heat to medium and bring to a boil. Stir well.
✦ Add the asparagus stems, reduce the heat to low and simmer, covered, for 5 minutes.
✦ Bring the stock to a boil in a small saucepan.
✦ Add the rice and 1 cup of the boiling stock to the onion, fennel and wine mixture, then bring to a boil over medium heat, stirring well. Reduce the heat to

low and simmer, uncovered, until the rice has absorbed all of the stock, about 10 minutes. Stir well.
✦ Add the remaining boiling stock and bring the mixture to a boil over medium heat, stirring well. Then sprinkle the asparagus tips over the rice, reduce the heat to low and simmer, uncovered, until the rice has absorbed all of the stock and is tender, about 10 minutes.
✦ Turn the heat off. Stir in the grated cheese and let stand over the heat source for 1 minute.
✦ Serve in individual bowls, sprinkled with the pine nuts and thin shavings of Parmesan cheese.

PER SERVING
469 calories/1964 kilojoules; 12 g protein; 17 g fat, 33% of calories (6.9 g saturated, 13.5% of calories; 6.2 g monounsaturated, 11.9%; 3.9 g polyunsaturated, 7.6%); 57 g carbohydrate; 6.8 g dietary fiber; 244 mg sodium; 1.7 mg iron; 22 mg cholesterol.

Tagliatelle with Garlic, Tomatoes, Olives and Capers
TAGLIATELLE ALLA PUTTANESCA

SERVES 4

1 red chili
*2 oz (60 g) canned anchovy
    fillets, drained*
2 tablespoons milk
1 tablespoon virgin olive oil
2 garlic cloves, crushed
*1½ cups (1 lb/500 g) chopped,
    vine-ripened tomatoes*
1 tablespoon capers
*12 black olives, pitted and
    halved*
*1 tablespoon chopped oregano
    or parsley*
10 oz (300 g) tagliatelle

The literal translation of this recipe title is "as a prostitute would prepare tagliatelle." This sauce is said to have been prepared and enjoyed by the Neapolitan ladies of the night. It is quick to prepare and tastes delicious.

PREPARATION   *10 minutes*
✦ Deseed and finely chop the chili.
✦ Rinse the anchovy fillets in the milk and pat dry.

COOKING   *20 minutes*
✦ Heat the oil in a medium-sized, non-stick skillet. Add the garlic and chili and sauté for 1 minute over medium heat.
✦ Add the anchovies and stir over low heat until the anchovies are soft, about 2 minutes.
✦ Add the tomatoes, capers, olives and oregano. Bring to a boil, then reduce the heat to low and simmer for 15 minutes.

✦ Meanwhile, bring a large saucepan of water to a boil. Add the tagliatelle and cook until just tender, about 10 minutes. Drain well.
✦ Divide the tagliatelle among 4 pasta bowls and pour the hot sauce over it. Serve immediately.

PER SERVING
358 calories/1498 kilojoules; 14 g protein; 7.6 g fat, 20% of calories (1.8 g saturated, 4.8% of calories; 3.9 g monounsaturated, 10.2%; 1.9 g polyunsaturated, 5%); 57 g carbohydrate; 5.7 g dietary fiber; 919 mg sodium; 1.7 mg iron; 12 mg cholesterol.

Risotto with Fennel and Asparagus

Spaghetti with Neapolitan Tomato Sauce

SPAGHETTI SALSA DI POMODORO ALLA NAPOLETANA

Naples is the center of pasta-making in southern Italy and spaghetti is the most popular shape. This famous sauce was developed for the Neapolitan pizza! Here it is served on spaghetti and topped with shrimp, snow peas and arugula.

SERVES 4

NEAPOLITAN SAUCE

1¾ cups (13 oz/410 g) canned
    plum (Roma) tomatoes with
    their juice
1 tablespoon virgin olive oil
1 onion, finely chopped
1 garlic clove, crushed
3 tablespoons tomato paste
1 teaspoon chopped oregano
1 teaspoon chopped basil
1 bay leaf
1 teaspoon sugar
¼ teaspoon salt
freshly ground black pepper,
    to taste

8 jumbo (large) raw shrimp
    (prawns)
8 oz (250 g) spaghetti
16 small snow peas (mange-tout)
1 cup arugula (rocket) leaves

PREPARATION   *15 minutes*
◆ Chop the tomatoes with kitchen scissors, retaining all of the juice.
◆ Shell and devein the shrimp and refrigerate until required.

COOKING   *30 minutes*
◆ Heat the oil in a medium-sized, heavy-bottomed saucepan over low heat. Add the onion and cook, stirring frequently, until the onion is soft but not brown, about 5 minutes. Add the garlic and cook, stirring, for 1 minute. Add the tomatoes and their juice to the pan.
◆ Add the tomato paste, herbs, sugar, salt and pepper, stirring well. Bring to a boil, then cover, reduce the heat and simmer for 20 minutes, stirring occasionally. Remove the bay leaf and discard.
◆ Meanwhile, bring a large saucepan of water to a boil. Add the spaghetti, stir well, then boil rapidly for 10 minutes, or until just tender. Drain and keep hot.

◆ While the pasta is cooking, bring a medium-sized saucepan of water to a boil. Add the shrimp, reduce the heat and simmer, just until the shrimp turn pink, about 3 to 5 minutes. Drain immediately.
◆ Place the snow peas in a plastic bag and twist to seal. Cook in a microwave oven on High for 1 minute. Alternatively, steam the snow peas until tender-crisp.
◆ To serve, divide the spaghetti among 4 pasta bowls. Spoon the tomato sauce over the spaghetti, then scatter the snow peas over the sauce. Top each serving with 2 of the shrimp and a quarter of the arugula.

PER SERVING
321 calories/1343 kilojoules; 17 g protein; 4.8 g fat, 14% of calories (0.95 g saturated, 2.8% of calories; 2.9 g monounsaturated, 8.4%; 0.95 g polyunsaturated, 2.8%); 51 g carbohydrate; 5.6 g dietary fiber; 387 mg sodium; 2 mg iron; 57 mg cholesterol.

Fettuccine with Basil Sauce

FETTUCCINE AL PESTO

Pesto sauce, the invention of the Ligurians, is one of the most famous pasta sauces to have come out of Italy. It features the sweet basil herb, and is traditionally served over fettuccine or trenette, a fine spaghetti-shaped pasta.

SERVES 4

PESTO SAUCE

¼ cup (1 oz/30 g) pine nuts
2 cups tightly packed basil leaves
¼ cup (2 fl oz/60 ml) extra
    virgin olive oil
2 garlic cloves, halved
½ cup (2 oz/60 g) freshly
    grated Parmesan cheese

10 oz (300 g) fresh fettuccine
basil leaves, for garnish

PREPARATION   *10 minutes*
◆ Preheat the broiler (grill).
◆ Toast the pine nuts under the broiler, stirring once, until golden, about 2 to 3 minutes.

COOKING   *15 minutes*
◆ Bring a large saucepan of water to a boil. Add the fettuccine and cook until just tender, about 5 minutes. Drain well, reserving a little of the pasta water.
◆ Meanwhile, make the pesto sauce. Place the basil leaves, oil, garlic and pine nuts in a blender (or a food processor fitted with a metal blade) and blend until a thick paste is formed. Stop and scrape down the sides when necessary, to combine well.
◆ Add ¼ cup of the Parmesan cheese and blend well.

◆ Return the pasta to the saucepan, add half the pesto sauce and toss to coat. Add some pasta water, a tablespoon at a time, until the pasta is coated lightly and evenly with pesto sauce.
◆ Divide the dressed pasta among 4 pasta bowls. Top with the remaining pesto sauce and garnish with the basil. Serve with the remaining grated Parmesan cheese.

PER SERVING
413 calories/1727 kilojoules; 12 g protein; 28 g fat, 61% of calories (5.8 g saturated, 12.8% of calories; 15.7 g monounsaturated, 34.2%; 6.5 g polyunsaturated, 14%); 29 g carbohydrate; 2.2 g dietary fiber; 245 mg sodium; 1.4 mg iron; 101 mg cholesterol.

Spaghetti with Neapolitan Tomato Sauce

Mushroom Risotto

RISOTTO CON FUNGHI

SERVES 4

*8 oz (250 g) wild field
  mushrooms or mushroom caps*
*3 tablespoons (1½ oz/45 g)
  butter*
1 small onion, finely chopped
*½ cup (4 fl oz/125 ml) dry
  white wine*
*4 cups (32 fl oz/1 l) vegetable
  stock*
*2 cups (12 oz/375 g) Precooked
  Rice for Risotto, see
  recipe below*
*¼ cup (1 oz/30 g) freshly grated
  Parmesan cheese*
flat-leaf parsley, for garnish

This recipe hails from northern Italy, a region known for its fresh wild mushrooms. To give this dish extra flavor, place an Italian black truffle in a jar with the raw rice a week before cooking.

PREPARATION   *10 minutes plus precooking of rice*
◆ Trim the stalks of the mushrooms. Then brush the mushrooms clean with a dry pastry brush and slice thinly.

COOKING   *20 minutes*
◆ Melt half the butter in a large, non-stick saucepan over low heat. Add the onion and cook, stirring continuously, for 3 minutes.
◆ Add the mushrooms and stir well. Add the wine and bring to a boil over medium heat, then simmer until all the wine evaporates, about 5 minutes.
◆ Bring the stock to a boil in a small saucepan, then add the stock and the precooked rice to the pan with the mushrooms. Return the mixture to a boil, stirring continuously. Reduce the heat to low and simmer, uncovered, until the stock has been absorbed and the rice is tender, about 5 to 7 minutes.
◆ Add the remaining butter and stir well.
◆ Serve in individual bowls, sprinkled with the Parmesan cheese and garnished with the parsley.

PER SERVING
*423 calories/1770 kilojoules; 11 g protein; 14 g fat,
30% of calories (7.9 g saturated, 16.9% of calories;
5.1 g monounsaturated, 10.9%; 1 g polyunsaturated, 2.2%);
59 g carbohydrate; 3.9 g dietary fiber; 224 mg sodium;
0.9 mg iron; 27 mg cholesterol.*

Precooked Rice for Risotto

RISO PRECOTTO

MAKES 6 CUPS

1 onion
8 cloves
1 tablespoon virgin olive oil
*2 cups (14 oz/440 g) Arborio
  rice*
*2 cups (16 fl oz/500 ml)
  vegetable stock*

This method for precooking rice for risotto was developed by a famous Italian chef to help cut down on the cooking time and attention required in the classic risotto method. Fortunately, none of the authentic flavor or texture is lost.

PREPARATION   *5 minutes*
◆ Peel the onion, then stick with the cloves.
◆ Preheat the oven to 450°F (230°C).

COOKING   *20 minutes*
◆ Heat the oil in a heavy-bottomed, flameproof casserole dish over low heat. Add the onion and cook for 4 minutes, adjusting the heat so that the onion does not brown.
◆ Add the rice and stir over medium heat until it is lightly browned, about 5 minutes.
◆ Bring the stock to a boil in a small saucepan, then add to the casserole dish, stirring well. Cover and bake for 8 minutes.
◆ Remove the onion and discard.
◆ Cool the rice mixture, then store in the refrigerator until required. The precooked rice will keep for up to 4 days in the refrigerator. Freeze for longer storage.

PER CUP
*263 calories/1100 kilojoules; 5 g protein; 2.8 g fat, 10% of
calories (0.6 g saturated, 2.1% of calories; 1.8 g monounsaturated,
6.4%; 0.4 g polyunsaturated, 1.5%); 54 g carbohydrate;
1.8 g dietary fiber; 16 mg sodium; 0.6 mg iron; 0 mg cholesterol.*

Agnolotti in Tomato Sauce

AGNOLOTTI ALLA PIEDMONTESE

The traditional Piedmont cuisine is rich in flavors and quite heavy. In this recipe, "lightened" to fit into today's healthy lifestyle, spinach filling is complemented with a tomato sauce. Fresh pasta is available in sheets from pasta shops.

SERVES 6

FILLING

2 tablespoons chopped, canned anchovy fillets or 2 tablespoons truffles
2 tablespoons milk, if using anchovies
2 teaspoons butter
2 teaspoons virgin olive oil
1 small onion, finely chopped
1 garlic clove, crushed
2 cups (16 fl oz/500 ml) water
2 cups (5½ oz/175 g) tightly packed, shredded spinach
¼ cup (1 oz/30 g) finely grated Parmesan cheese
freshly ground black pepper, to taste

2 sheets rolled fresh pasta, 12 × 14 in (30 × 35 cm), about 6½ oz (200 g)
water or egg white, for sealing the agnolotti
oregano sprigs, for garnish

SAUCE

1 tablespoon virgin olive oil
1 onion, finely chopped
2 garlic cloves, crushed
1½ cups (1 lb/500 g) chopped, plum (Roma) tomatoes
½ cup (4 fl oz/125 ml) water
½ cup (4 fl oz/125 ml) dry white wine
¼ cup drained, sliced sun-dried tomatoes packed in oil
2 tablespoons chopped oregano
¼ teaspoon salt
¼ teaspoon freshly ground black pepper

PREPARATION   *40 minutes*

♦ If using anchovies, soak them in the milk for 10 minutes to wash off the excess salt. Drain and pat dry.

COOKING   *1 hour and 20 minutes*

♦ To make the filling, heat the butter and oil in a small skillet over low heat. Add the onion and garlic and cook gently until the onion is soft and transparent, about 5 minutes. Transfer to a mixing bowl.

♦ Bring the water to a boil in a medium-sized saucepan, add the spinach, then remove from the heat and let stand for 1 minute. Drain well. Cool the spinach until you can handle it with your hands, about 5 minutes, then squeeze out all of the excess liquid.

♦ Add the spinach, anchovies, Parmesan cheese and pepper to the onion mixture. Mix together well.

♦ On one sheet of the pasta, place teaspoons of the filling in little heaps at 1½ in (3 cm) intervals, making 6 rows each of 6 heaps of filling.

♦ Brush the spaces between the filling with the water or egg white. Cover with the second sheet of pasta and press with the fingers around each heap of filling to seal. Cut around the enclosed heaps with a pasta wheel or sharp knife, making 36 agnolotti squares. Squeeze the edges together firmly and set aside.

♦ To make the sauce, heat the oil in a large saucepan over medium heat. Add the onion and garlic and sauté, stirring frequently, for 5 minutes.

♦ Add the plum tomatoes, water and half of the wine. Bring to a boil, then reduce the heat and simmer, uncovered, for 20 minutes.

♦ Place the mixture in a food processor fitted with a metal blade and mix for 10 seconds to create a textured sauce.

♦ Return the tomato mixture to the saucepan. Add the remaining wine, sundried tomatoes, oregano, salt and pepper. Return to a boil, stirring occasionally, then remove from the heat and keep warm.

♦ Bring a large saucepan of water to a boil. Add 12 of the agnolotti, reduce the heat to medium-high, and cook until the pasta is just tender, about 5 to 8 minutes. Remove with a slotted spoon and keep hot. Repeat with the remaining agnolotti.

♦ Divide the agnolotti among 6 pasta bowls, top with the hot tomato sauce and garnish with the oregano sprigs. Serve with a bowl of freshly grated Parmesan cheese for sprinkling on top, if desired.

PER SERVING

262 calories/1097 kilojoules; 11 g protein; 11 g fat, 39% of calories (3.7 g saturated, 13.3% of calories; 5.5 g monounsaturated, 19.5%; 1.8 g polyunsaturated, 6.2%); 26 g carbohydrate; 3.7 g dietary fiber; 571 mg sodium; 2.4 mg iron; 75 mg cholesterol.

Italian markets carry a large variety of fresh fruit and vegetables.

"Little Hats" Stuffed with Cheese

CAPPELLETTI DI ROMAGNA

Cappelletti, like tortellini, are shaped like the beautiful navel of Venus. According to legend, they were created by a cook in Castelfranco who saw Venus alone in her naked glory and created the tortellini to immortalize the moment.

SERVES 6

SAUCE

8 porcini mushrooms (cèpes)
2 teaspoons butter
2 garlic cloves, crushed
4 oz (125 g) mushrooms, finely chopped
2 tablespoons shredded mint
1 cup (8 fl oz/250 ml) dry white wine
½ cup (4 fl oz/125 ml) vegetable or chicken stock, skimmed of fat
½ cup (4 fl oz/125 ml) light cream
freshly ground black pepper, to taste
4 thin slices Italian salami, cut into julienne strips, optional

FILLING

½ cup (4 oz/125 g) ricotta cheese
⅓ cup (1½ oz/45 g) crumbled Gorgonzola cheese
¼ cup (1 oz/30 g) freshly grated Parmesan cheese
½ cup (4 oz/125 g) diced, cooked chicken breast
½ teaspoon ground nutmeg
2 tablespoons shredded mint

2 sheets rolled fresh pasta, 12 × 14 in (30 × 35 cm), about 6½ oz (200 g)
water or egg white, for sealing the cappelletti
mint sprigs, for garnish

PREPARATION   *30 minutes*

◆ If using dried porcini mushroms, soak them in boiling water for 5 minutes, then drain and chop finely.

COOKING   *50 minutes*

◆ To make the filling, place the ricotta, Gorgonzola and Parmesan cheeses in a small, mixing bowl. Add the chicken, nutmeg and mint and combine well with a fork.

◆ Cut out thirty-six 2 in (5 cm) circles of pasta with a pastry cutter. Place a teaspoon of filling on each circle. Brush the edges with the water or egg white, fold in half and pinch to seal well.

◆ Roll the sealed edges over to form a "cuff." Brush the ends of the half circles with water. Hold the straight edge of a half circle over the tip of your index finger, then wrap gently around the finger and pinch the ends together. Continue until all of the cappelletti are shaped.

◆ To make the sauce, heat the butter in a medium-sized saucepan over low heat. Add the garlic and mushrooms and sauté gently, stirring occasionally, for 5 minutes. Add the mint and the chopped porcini mushrooms to the saucepan and stir.

◆ Add the wine, stock and cream and bring to a boil. Reduce the heat to low and simmer for 5 minutes to reduce the sauce. Stir in the pepper and salami, if using, and keep warm.

◆ Bring a large saucepan of water to a boil. Add 12 of the cappelletti, reduce the heat to medium-high and cook until the pasta is just tender, about 5 to 8 minutes. Remove with a slotted spoon and keep hot. Repeat with the remaining cappelletti.

◆ Divide the cappelletti among 6 pasta bowls, top with the hot sauce and garnish with the mint sprigs. Serve with a bowl of freshly grated Parmesan cheese for sprinkling on top, if desired.

PER SERVING (WITHOUT SALAMI)
320 calories/1338 kilojoules; 15 g protein; 17 g fat, 47% of calories (10.3 g saturated, 28.7% of calories; 5.4 g monounsaturated, 15%; 1.3 g polyunsaturated, 3.3%); 20 g carbohydrate; 1.9 g dietary fiber; 331 mg sodium; 0.9 mg iron; 112 mg cholesterol.

This Italian food store stocks an amazing variety of cheeses.

"Little Hats" Stuffed with Cheese

Rice and Cheese Croquettes

SUPPLI AL TELEFONO

SERVES 6

2 cups Risotto with Saffron, see
    recipe below
1½ oz (50 g) reduced-fat
    mozzarella cheese
2 large eggs
¼ cup (1 oz/30 g) dry bread
    crumbs, firmly packed
about 3 cups vegetable oil, for
    deep-frying

This is a delicious use for leftover risotto! Risotto with Saffron (see recipe below) is wrapped around mozzarella, then coated and deep-fried to produce these croquettes. Italian children love them and they are often served as a snack.

PREPARATION   *60 minutes including making risotto*
◆ Chill the risotto.
◆ Cut the cheese into 12 equal-sized cubes.
◆ Line an ovenproof casserole dish with paper towels.

COOKING   *1 hour*
◆ Beat the eggs with a fork in a medium-sized bowl until smooth. Add the cold risotto mixture, and stir well with a fork.
◆ Divide the mixture into 12 equal portions. Place a cube of cheese in the middle of a portion and, with cool, clean hands, press together and mold into a ball. Continue shaping all of the croquettes in this manner.
◆ Place the bread crumbs in a bowl. Roll each rice ball in the bread crumbs, then place on a square of wax (greaseproof) paper on a plate.
◆ Chill in the refrigerator for at least 30 minutes.

◆ Preheat the oven to 250°F (120°C).
◆ Re-roll the croquettes into shape, if necessary, after chilling.
◆ Heat the oil in a deep-fryer or a deep saucepan to 350°F (180°C).
◆ Deep-fry the croquettes, 6 at a time, until golden brown and hot in the center, about 5 minutes. Place in the casserole dish and keep warm in the oven. Repeat with the remaining croquettes.
◆ Serve within 10 minutes of frying for best results.

PER SERVING
286 calories/1198 kilojoules; 7 g protein; 19 g fat, 58% of calories (7 g saturated, 21.5% of calories; 5.9 g monounsaturated, 17.9%; 6.1 g polyunsaturated, 18.6%); 22 g carbohydrate; 0.9 g dietary fiber; 163 mg sodium; 0.6 mg iron; 80 mg cholesterol.

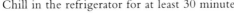

Risotto with Saffron

RISOTTO ALLA MILANESE

SERVES 8

¼ teaspoon saffron threads
2 tablespoons water
½ cup (4 oz/125 g) unsalted
    butter
1 onion, chopped
¼ teaspoon freshly ground black
    pepper
2 cups (16 fl oz/500 ml) dry
    white wine
2½ cups (17½ oz/550 g)
    Arborio rice
pinch salt
2½ cups (20 fl oz/625 ml)
    chicken stock, skimmed of fat,
    plus extra if required
1½ cups (6 oz/185 g) freshly
    grated Parmesan cheese, plus
    extra for serving

Risotto is the name given to dishes cooked with rices like Arborio and Canaroli—they have plumper grains than long-grain rice, and give risotto its characteristic creaminess. There are many versions of risotto, but this is considered a classic.

PREPARATION   *15 minutes*
◆ Soak the saffron in the water for 15 minutes.

COOKING   *1 hour*
◆ Melt two-thirds of the butter in a large, heavy-bottomed saucepan over low heat. Add the onion and pepper and cook until the onion is golden brown, about 5 minutes.
◆ Add the wine and simmer until the liquid has reduced by half, about 10 minutes.
◆ Add the rice and the salt and cook, stirring continuously, until the wine has been absorbed, about 3 minutes. Add the saffron with its liquid and enough of the chicken stock to cover the rice. Cook gently, stirring continuously, until all of the liquid has been absorbed, about 10 to 15 minutes.

◆ Add the remaining stock in small amounts, adding more only as each quantity is absorbed. Use just enough stock so that the rice is cooked until tender but is still firm, and stir often to prevent the rice from sticking.
◆ Remove from the heat and stir in the remaining butter and the Parmesan cheese. Serve hot, with extra Parmesan.

PER SERVING
517 calories/2164 kilojoules; 15 g protein; 21.5 g fat, 37% of calories (13.6 g saturated, 23.3% of calories; 6.6 g monounsaturated, 11.5%; 1.3 g polyunsaturated, 2.2%); 56 g carbohydrate; 1.8 g dietary fiber; 539.5 mg sodium; 0.75 mg iron; 59.5 mg cholesterol.

*Risotto with Saffron and
Rice and Cheese Croquettes (right)*

Sardinian Ravioli with Cheese Stuffing and Red Pepper Sauce

CULINGIONES

This adaptation of a ravioli recipe from the rugged but beautiful island of Sardinia (the second-largest island in the Mediterranean) features goat cheese and a light and bright red pepper sauce.

SERVES 6

SAUCE
1 lb (500 g) red bell peppers
    (capsicum)
1 tablespoon virgin olive oil
1 onion, finely chopped
½ cup (4 fl oz / 125 ml) dry
    white wine or grape juice

FILLING
¾ cup (3¼ oz / 100 g) crumbled
    goat cheese
¼ cup (1 oz / 30 g) freshly
    grated Parmesan cheese
¼ cup finely chopped, drained
    preserved artichoke hearts
¼ teaspoon ground nutmeg
¼ teaspoon ground turmeric

2 sheets rolled fresh pasta,
    12 × 14 in (30 × 35 cm),
    about 6½ oz (200 g)
water or egg white, for sealing
    ravioli
basil leaves, for garnish

PREPARATION   *30 minutes*
+ Preheat the broiler (grill).
+ Cut the bell peppers in half lengthwise and remove the seeds and white membrane. Broil (grill) the bell pepper halves until the skin is charred and blistered, about 5 minutes. Place the peppers in a clean, plastic bag, seal, cover with a cloth and leave for 5 minutes. Rub the skin off the pepper halves with your fingers.

COOKING   *50 minutes*
+ Place all of the filling ingredients in a bowl and mix well with a fork.
+ On one sheet of the pasta, place teaspoons of the filling in little heaps at 1½ in (3 cm) intervals, making 6 rows each of 6 heaps of filling.
+ Brush the spaces between the filling with the water or egg white. Cover with the second sheet of pasta and press with the fingers around each heap of filling to seal. Cut around the enclosed heaps with a pasta wheel or sharp knife, making 36 ravioli squares. Squeeze the edges together firmly.
+ Set aside and prepare the sauce.

+ Heat the oil in a medium-sized saucepan over low heat. Add the onion and sauté, stirring occasionally, until soft, about 5 minutes. Add the prepared red peppers and wine and bring to a boil.
+ Place the mixture in a food processor fitted with a metal blade and purée. Return the mixture to the pan and keep hot.
+ Bring a large saucepan of water to a boil. Add 12 of the ravioli and cook over medium-high heat until the pasta is just tender, about 5 to 8 minutes. Remove with a slotted spoon and keep hot. Repeat with the remaining ravioli.
+ Divide the hot sauce among 6 plates, arrange 6 hot ravioli on top of the sauce and serve, garnished with the basil leaves.

PER SERVING
274 calories / 1145 kilojoules; 13 g protein; 13 g fat,
42% of calories (6.4 g saturated, 20.6% of calories;
5.3 g monounsaturated, 17.2%; 1.3 g polyunsaturated, 4.2%);
23 g carbohydrate; 2.5 g dietary fiber; 308 mg sodium; 1 mg iron;
84 mg cholesterol.

Sardinian Ravioli with
Cheese Stuffing and Red Pepper Sauce

Butternut Squash Risotto
RISOTTO CON LA ZUCCA

Risotto often replaces pasta in Piedmont and Lombardy, the regions of northern Italy where it originated. The Milanese are especially fond of risotto as a late night supper dish, often after the theater.

SERVES 4

1 lb (500 g) butternut squash (butternut pumpkin), peeled and seeded

2 tablespoons (1 oz/30 g) butter

1 tablespoon virgin olive oil, garlic-flavored if available

1 onion, finely chopped

½ cup (4 fl oz/125 ml) dry white wine

½ cup (4 fl oz/125 ml) water

2 cups (16 fl oz/500 ml) vegetable or chicken stock, skimmed of fat

1¼ cups (8½ oz/275 g) Arborio rice

¼ cup (1 oz/30 g) freshly grated Parmesan cheese

2 tablespoons shredded mint

mint sprigs, for garnish

PREPARATION   *15 minutes*
- Cut the butternut squash into ½ in (1 cm) chunks.

COOKING   *55 minutes*
- In a large, heavy-bottomed saucepan, heat the butter and oil over medium heat. Add the onion, reduce the heat to low, cover and cook, occasionally shaking the pan from side to side while still in contact with the heat, for 5 minutes.
- Meanwhile, bring the wine and water to a boil in a small saucepan.
- Add the butternut squash and the boiling wine and water to the saucepan with the onion and stir well. Cover and cook over low heat until the squash is tender, about 15 minutes.
- While the squash is cooking, bring the stock to a boil in a small saucepan.
- Stir the rice into the squash mixture. Add 1 cup of the boiling stock. Increase the heat to medium and when bubbles appear, reduce the heat to low and cook, uncovered, until all the liquid is absorbed, about 10 minutes.

- Add the remaining boiling stock, stir well, and continue cooking in this manner, until the rice has again absorbed all the liquid and is tender, an additional 10 to 15 minutes. Turn the heat off, but leave the pan on the heat source.
- Gently stir in half of the Parmesan cheese and all of the shredded mint, and let stand for 1 minute.
- Serve in individual bowls, sprinkled with the remaining Parmesan cheese and garnished with the mint sprigs.

PER SERVING
426 calories/1781 kilojoules; 10 g protein; 13 g fat, 29% of calories (6.9 g saturated, 15.4% of calories; 5.2 g monounsaturated, 11.6%; 0.9 g polyunsaturated, 2%); 61 g carbohydrate; 3.5 g dietary fiber; 188 mg sodium; 1.1 mg iron; 22 mg cholesterol.

An outdoor eating area at Camogli on the Italian Riviera.

Butternut Squash Risotto

Tomatoes Stuffed with Rice
POMODORI CON RISO

SERVES 4

3 cups (24 fl oz/750 ml) water
½ cup (3½ oz/110 g) Arborio
 rice
4 large, vine-ripened tomatoes
1 tablespoon virgin olive oil
1 cup thinly sliced leeks
2 garlic cloves, crushed
1 tablespoon capers
4 anchovy fillets, chopped
4 tablespoons shredded basil
4 sundried tomatoes packed in
 oil, well drained and sliced
⅓ cup (1¼ oz/40 g) freshly
 grated Parmesan cheese
1 cup (8 fl oz/250 ml)
 vegetable stock

Use large vine-ripened tomatoes for good flavor and Italian Arborio rice for authenticity in this delicious Neapolitan dish. In summer it may be served cold as a refreshing appetizer but it tastes just as good served hot.

PREPARATION   *15 minutes*
◆ Bring the water to a boil in a large saucepan, then add the rice. Boil for 10 minutes. Drain well.
◆ Cut a slice off the end of each tomato, opposite the stalk end, and reserve. Scoop out the pulp and reserve.
◆ Preheat the oven to 350°F (180°C).

COOKING   *30 minutes*
◆ Heat the oil in a small skillet over low heat. Add the leeks and cook, stirring frequently, for 5 minutes. Add the garlic and fry for an additional minute.
◆ Place the leek mixture in a large bowl. Add the cooked rice, tomato pulp, capers, anchovies, basil, sundried tomatoes and Parmesan cheese. Mix well.
◆ Place the tomato shells in a shallow baking dish.

Spoon the rice mixture evenly into the tomatoes, pressing down carefully so that they are generously filled.
◆ Bring the stock to a boil in a small saucepan.
◆ Pour the stock around the tomatoes and bake until the tomatoes are soft when tested with a skewer, about 20 minutes.
◆ Place on a serving dish and serve.

PER SERVING
224 calories/939 kilojoules; 9 g protein; 8.9 g fat, 36% of calories (3.1 g saturated, 12.6% of calories; 4.1 g monounsaturated, 16.6%; 1.7 g polyunsaturated, 6.8%); 27 g carbohydrate; 3.5 g dietary fiber; 362 mg sodium; 1 mg iron; 12 mg cholesterol.

Braised Rice and Peas
RISI E BISI

SERVES 6

2 lb (1 kg) peas, in the shell
3 tablespoons (1½ oz/45 g)
 butter
1 onion, finely chopped
4 cups (32 fl oz/1 l) chicken
 stock, skimmed of fat, plus
 extra if required
1¾ cups (12¾ oz/385 g)
 Arborio rice
1 cup (8 oz/250 g) diced ham
½ cup (2 oz/60 g) freshly grated
 Parmesan cheese

Risi e Bisi is a famous dish from Venice. It is best in springtime when the fresh peas are sweet and tender. It is like a risotto, though its consistency is more liquid, more like that of a soup.

PREPARATION   *20 minutes*
Shell the peas.

COOKING   *30 minutes*
◆ Melt 2 tablespoons of the butter in a large, heavy-bottomed saucepan over medium heat. Add the onion and cook, stirring frequently, until soft and transparent but not brown, about 3 minutes.
◆ Bring the stock to a boil in a small saucepan.
◆ Meanwhile, add the rice, ham and peas to the saucepan with the onion and cook, stirring continuously, for 2 minutes.
◆ Add 2 cups of the boiling stock to the rice mixture, reduce the heat to low-medium and stir well. Simmer, uncovered, stirring occasionally, until almost all of the stock is absorbed, about 10 minutes.
◆ Add another cup of the boiling stock and simmer,

stirring occasionally, until the stock is again absorbed, about 5 minutes. Add the remaining stock and simmer for an additional 5 minutes, stirring occasionally, until the rice and peas are tender. If the rice is not cooked, continue adding more boiling stock, ¼ cup at a time, and simmer until tender.
◆ Add the remaining butter and the grated Parmesan cheese and combine well.
◆ Serve immediately in pasta bowls or wide soup plates.

PER SERVING
403 calories/1689 kilojoules; 18 g protein; 10 g fat, 23% of calories (6.4 g saturated, 14.7% of calories; 3 g monounsaturated, 6.9%; 0.6 g polyunsaturated, 1.4%); 59 g carbohydrate; 5.6 g dietary fiber; 789 mg sodium; 2.4 mg iron; 36 mg cholesterol.

Tomatoes Stuffed with Rice

Stir-Fried Noodles with Chicken

GWAYTEOW PAHT GAI

SERVES 4

8 oz (250 g) rice noodles (rice
  vermicelli)
1 tablespoon peanut oil
1 garlic clove, crushed
4 oz (125 g) chicken breast
  fillet, thinly sliced
1 large egg, lightly beaten
4 scallions (spring onions),
  chopped
1 teaspoon chopped pickled
  radish
1 teaspoon palm or brown sugar
1 tablespoon fish sauce
1 tablespoon reduced-sodium
  soy sauce
2 tablespoons coarsely chopped
  cilantro (coriander)

Noodles are seldom served plain in Thailand—they are usually mixed with chicken, pork or shrimp, vegetables and flavorings to produce a tasty satisfying dish. Pickled radishes and fish sauce are available at specialty Asian food stores.

PREPARATION   *20 minutes*
✦ Place the noodles in a large bowl, add enough hot water to cover and leave to soak for 15 minutes. Drain.

COOKING   *15 minutes*
✦ Heat the oil in a wok or large, heavy-bottomed skillet over medium-high heat. Add the garlic and chicken and stir-fry until the chicken is cooked through, about 3 minutes.
✦ Add the egg and scallions and stir quickly until the egg sets, about 1 to 2 minutes.
✦ Add the pickled radish, sugar, and fish and soy sauces, and stir-fry for 1 minute.

✦ Add the noodles, reduce the heat to medium and cook, stirring continuously, until the noodles are heated through, about 3 to 5 minutes.
✦ Place in a large serving bowl or in individual bowls, sprinkle the cilantro on top and serve immediately.

PER SERVING
330 calories / 1383 kilojoules; 13 g protein; 6.3 g fat, 18% of calories (1.6 g saturated, 4.5% of calories; 2.9 g monounsaturated, 8.3%; 1.8 g polyunsaturated, 5.2%); 53 g carbohydrate; 0.2 g dietary fiber; 303 mg sodium; 1.5 mg iron; 72 mg cholesterol.

Fried Rice with Chicken and Curry

KHAO PAHT KAH-REE GAI

SERVES 4

3 cups (24 fl oz / 750 ml) water
1 cup (7 oz / 220 g) jasmine or
  other long-grain rice
2 tablespoons peanut oil
2 garlic cloves, crushed
2 teaspoons curry paste or curry
  powder
4 oz (125 g) chicken breast
  fillet, chopped
1 tablespoon reduced-sodium
  soy sauce
1 tablespoon fish sauce
½ teaspoon palm or brown sugar
2 scallions (spring onions),
  thinly sliced
2 tablespoons coarsely chopped
  cilantro (coriander)

Fried rice has universal appeal as an accompaniment or as a tasty snack. This Thai version is quick and easy. If you prefer, cook the rice a day in advance—in fact, in Thailand fried rice is made with rice left over from the previous night.

PREPARATION   *10 minutes plus 1 hour cooling time*
✦ Bring the water to a boil in a medium-sized saucepan. Add the rice and boil rapidly for 10 minutes, then remove from the heat. Drain and rinse the rice under cold, running water. Place in a colander and let cool, covered, for at least 1 hour.

COOKING   *10 minutes*
✦ Heat the oil in a wok over medium-high heat. Add the garlic and curry paste and stir-fry for 1 minute. Add the chicken and stir-fry until it is cooked through, about 3 minutes.

✦ Add the rice, soy and fish sauces, sugar and scallions, reduce the heat to medium and cook, stirring continuously, until the rice is hot, about 5 minutes.
✦ Place in a large serving bowl, sprinkle the cilantro on top and serve immediately.

PER SERVING
270 calories / 1129 kilojoules; 11 g protein; 8.9 g fat, 30% of calories (2 g saturated, 6.6% of calories; 4 g monounsaturated, 13.5%; 2.9 g polyunsaturated, 9.9%); 36 g carbohydrate; 1.4 g dietary fiber; 220 mg sodium; 2.2 mg iron; 16 mg cholesterol.

Stir-Fried Noodles with Chicken

Crispy Rice Noodles

MEE GROB

SERVES 4

½ cup (1 oz/30 g) bean sprouts
¼ cup diagonally sliced scallions
  (spring onions)
1 small red chili, seeded and
  thinly sliced
4 tablespoons cilantro (coriander)
  leaves
2 garlic cloves, crushed
¼ cup (2 fl oz/60 ml) reduced-
  sodium chicken stock,
  skimmed of fat
4 oz (125 g) pork loin (fillet),
  thinly sliced
1 chicken breast fillet
  (about 4 oz/125 g), cut into
  thin strips
4 oz (125 g) tofu, cubed
2 tablespoons soybean paste
1 tablespoon rice vinegar
1 tablespoon palm or brown
  sugar
1 teaspoon fish sauce
3 cups (24 fl oz/750 ml)
  vegetable oil, for deep-frying
2 large eggs, beaten
6 oz (175 g) rice noodles
  (rice vermicelli)

Usually rice noodles are soaked before use, but in this dish they are deep-fried, and puff up to twice their original size. This satisfying dish should be enjoyed as soon as it is cooked so that the crisp texture of the noodles is not lost.

PREPARATION   *15 minutes*
♦ Place the bean sprouts, scallions, chili slices and cilantro leaves in separate serving bowls.

COOKING   *25 minutes*
♦ Place the garlic and stock in a wok or large, heavy-bottomed skillet and bring to a boil over medium heat. Add the pork and chicken and cook, stirring occasionally, for 3 minutes.
♦ Add the tofu, soybean paste, vinegar, sugar and fish sauce and simmer over low heat for 2 minutes. Remove the skillet from the heat and set aside.
♦ Heat 1 tablespoon of the oil in a small skillet over medium heat, add the beaten egg and cook gently, without stirring, until firm. Flip over and cook until golden. Slide the omelet onto a plate, roll up tightly and slice thinly to form strips.

♦ Heat the remaining oil in a wok. When a haze appears above the oil, add the noodles, in several batches, and deep-fry until crisp, about 1 minute per batch. Remove with a slotted spoon and drain well on paper towels.
♦ Return the skillet with the pork and chicken mixture to the heat source over medium heat. Add the crisp-fried noodles and the egg strips and cook, stirring continuously, until heated through, about 2 minutes.
♦ Serve immediately in individual bowls, accompanied by the bean sprouts, scallions, chili and cilantro for sprinkling on top of each portion.

PER SERVING
389 calories/1628 kilojoules; 24 g protein; 13 g fat, 31% of calories (1.8 g saturated, 4.3% of calories; 3.5 g monounsaturated, 8.4%; 7.7 g polyunsaturated, 18.3%); 43 g carbohydrate; 1.1 g dietary fiber; 432 mg sodium; 2.6 mg iron; 121 mg cholesterol.

A gilded statue of Kinnari, a mythical creature, in the grounds of the Grand Palace, Bangkok.

Rice Paper Rolls

GOI CUON

MAKES 12

4 oz (125 g) pork loin (fillet)
3 oz (90 g) rice noodles (rice vermicelli)
12 small round rice paper wrappers
12 small cooked shrimp (prawns), shelled, deveined and coarsely chopped
3 romaine (cos) lettuces leaves, shredded
½ cup (1 oz 30 g) bean sprouts
12 Vietnamese mint sprigs
freshly squeezed juice of 1 large lime
24 garlic chives
1 quantity nuoc cham sauce (see page 54)

Small rice paper rounds are filled with pork, shrimp, noodles, lettuce and fresh Vietnamese mint leaves, then rolled up and served with a spicy sauce for a tasty appetizer. Rice papers and soybean paste are available in specialty Asian stores.

PREPARATION   *30 minutes*
◆ Preheat the broiler (grill).

COOKING   *45 minutes*
◆ Broil the pork until it is no longer pink in the center, about 3 minutes on each side. Remove from the heat, cool and finely chop.
◆ Bring a large saucepan of water to a boil. Add the noodles and cook until tender, about 2 minutes. Drain, rinse well under cold, running water and drain again.
◆ Using a pastry brush, brush a rice paper wrapper carefully with warm water. Too much water will make the wrappers stick together. Place a second wrapper on top of the first one and brush it with warm water. Continue in the same manner with the remaining wrappers.
◆ Take a moist rice paper wrapper and place one-twelfth of the shrimp over the bottom third. Top with one-twelfth of each of the noodles, lettuce, pork and bean sprouts. Place the leaves from 1 Vietnamese mint sprig on top of the bean sprouts. Sprinkle with a little lime juice.
◆ Fold the bottom of the rice paper wrapper over the filling, then, holding the filling in place, fold both sides of the wrapper over tightly and roll up halfway. Place 2 garlic chives across the center of the wrapper, extending them beyond the edges of the wrapper and roll up tightly. Place the roll on a serving platter, with the seam side down. Continue making rolls with the remaining wrappers and filling ingredients.
◆ Serve the freshly made rolls with the nuoc cham sauce.

PER ROLL
73 calories / 305 kilojoules; 5 g protein; 1.1 g fat, 14% of calories (0.2 g saturated, 3% of calories; 0.5 g monounsaturated, 6%; 0.4 g polyunsaturated, 5%); 11 g carbohydrate; 0.4 g dietary fiber; 191 mg sodium; 1 mg iron; 11 mg cholesterol.

Paddy field, Vietnam. Rice is the country's major crop and it is also the foundation of most meals.

Sizzling Pancakes

BANH XEO

Filled with shrimp, pork and bean sprouts, these crispy pancakes are usually served as a first course but they can also be enjoyed as a light meal. Rice flour is sold in health food stores as well as in Asian specialty stores.

MAKES 10

NUOC CHAM SAUCE

1 small red chili, seeded and finely chopped
1 garlic clove, crushed
¼ cup (1½ oz/45 g) palm or brown sugar
2 teaspoons white vinegar
¼ cup (2 fl oz/60 ml) fish sauce
2 tablespoons lime juice
2 tablespoons grated carrot
¾ cup (6 fl oz/180 ml) warm water

PANCAKE BATTER

1¼ cups (7½ oz/235 g) rice flour
½ teaspoon curry powder
¼ teaspoon ground turmeric
½ cup (4 fl oz/125 ml) coconut milk
1½ cups (12 fl oz/375 ml) water
1 scallion (spring onion), thinly sliced

about ½ cup (4 fl oz/125 ml) vegetable oil
8 oz (250 g) pork loin (fillet), cut into julienne strips
8 oz (250 g) cooked small shrimp (prawns), shelled, deveined and halved lengthwise
10 small button mushrooms, thinly sliced
1 onion, cut into 10 thin slices
2 garlic cloves, crushed
2½ cups (5 oz/150 g) bean sprouts

PREPARATION   *30 minutes*

✦ To make the nuoc cham sauce, place all the ingredients except the water in a small bowl and stir well. Add the warm water and stir well.
✦ To make the pancake batter, place the rice flour, curry powder and turmeric in a medium-sized bowl. Make a well in the center, add the coconut milk and ½ cup of the water and beat with a wooden spoon until smooth. Stir in the remaining water and the scallion.
✦ Preheat the oven to 300°F (150°C).

COOKING   *1 hour*

✦ Heat 2 teapoons of the oil in a medium-sized, non-stick skillet over medium-high heat. Add one-tenth of the pork, shrimp and mushrooms, 1 onion slice and one-tenth of the garlic. Cook, stirring frequently, until the onion is soft and the pork is cooked, about 1 to 2 minutes.
✦ Increase the heat to high. Stir the batter well, then pour ⅓ cup of the batter into the skillet over the pork mixture (it should sizzle). Working quickly, tilt the skillet so that the batter flows to form an evenly thin pancake. Cover and cook until the edges curl up and the pancake is golden brown on the bottom, about 2 to 3 minutes.
✦ Slide the pancake onto a large plate. Keep warm in the oven while continuing to make pancakes using the remainder of the batter and filling ingredients, adding more oil to the pan when necessary, until you have 10 pancakes. Interleave the cooked pancakes with strips of waxed (greaseproof) paper as you add them to the ones in the oven.
✦ To serve, sprinkle ¼ cup of the bean sprouts over each pancake. Fold each pancake in half and serve on individual plates with the nuoc cham sauce drizzled on top.

PER PANCAKE

278 calories/1165 kilojoules; 14 g protein; 13 g fat, 42% of calories (3.2 g saturated, 10.5% of calories; 2.2 g mono-unsaturated, 7.1%; 7.6 g polyunsaturated, 24.4%); 26 g carbohydrate; 1.6 g dietary fiber; 279 mg sodium; 1 mg iron; 60 mg cholesterol.

A coastal village nestled among rugged hills in North Vietnam.

Sizzling Pancakes

Bulghur, Tomato, Mint and Parsley Salad

TABBOULEH

The Lebanese serve *tabbouleh* as part of an appetizer, or *mezze,* selection, and it is an essential ingredient in a *falafel* roll. Prepare this salad the day before serving and it will taste even better.

SERVES 8

⅔ cup (3¾ oz/115 g) bulghur
¼ cup finely sliced scallions
   (spring onions)
2 cups coarsely chopped
   flat-leaf parsley
¼ cup shredded mint
1 vine-ripened tomato, diced
¼ cup (1½ oz/45 g) thinly
   sliced radish, optional
¼ cup (2 fl oz/60 ml) extra
   virgin olive oil
⅓ cup (3 fl oz/90 ml) freshly
   squeezed lemon juice
generous pinch salt
¼ teaspoon freshly ground
   black pepper

PREPARATION *10 minutes plus 30 minutes soaking time*
✦ Place the bulghur in a medium-sized bowl, add enough cold water to cover and soak for 30 minutes. Drain well in a cheesecloth-lined sieve, then wrap in the cheesecloth and squeeze out any excess water.

ASSEMBLY *5 minutes*
✦ Place the bulghur in a large mixing bowl. Add all of the remaining ingredients. Combine well.

✦ Place the salad in a serving bowl and serve immediately, or cover with plastic wrap and chill until ready to serve.

PER SERVING
113 calories/472 kilojoules; 2 g protein; 7.4 g fat, 60% of calories (1.2 g saturated, 9.6% of calories; 5.3 g monounsaturated, 43.2%; 0.9 g polyunsaturated, 7.2%); 9 g carbohydrate; 3.4 g dietary fiber; 61 mg sodium; 1 mg iron; 0 mg cholesterol.

Bulghur and Pomegranate Salad

BURGHUL BI ROMAN MTABBLI

Olives, walnuts and pomegranate add a variety of textures and unique flavors to this salad. Serve it with grilled fish, barbecued chicken or lamb. Pomegranate molasses is available at Lebanese food stores. Light molasses can be substituted.

SERVES 8

⅔ cup (3¾ oz/115 g) bulghur
4 oz (125 g) large green Turkish
   or black kalamata olives,
   pitted and sliced
¼ cup (1 oz/30 g) chopped
   walnuts
8 scallions (spring onions),
   thinly sliced
½ cup coarsely chopped flat-leaf
   parsley
2 teaspoons pomegranate molasses
¼ teaspoon crushed red pepper
   (chili) flakes
2 tablespoons extra virgin olive oil
¼ cup (2 fl oz/60 ml) freshly
   squeezed lemon juice
¼ cup (2 fl oz/60 ml) freshly
   squeezed orange juice
1 cup fresh pomegranate seeds

PREPARATION *10 minutes plus 30 minutes soaking time*
✦ Place the bulghur in a medium-sized bowl, add enough cold water to cover and soak for 30 minutes. Drain well in a cheesecloth-lined sieve, then wrap in the cheesecloth and squeeze out any excess water.

ASSEMBLY *5 minutes plus at least 6 hours chilling time*
✦ Place the bulghur in a large mixing bowl. Add the remaining ingredients except the pomegranate seeds. Combine well.
✦ Cover the bowl and chill in the refrigerator for at least 6 hours, or preferably overnight to achieve the best flavor.

✦ Return the salad to room temperature. Just before serving, transfer to a serving bowl and fold in the pomegranate seeds.

PER SERVING
149 calories/624 kilojoules; 3 g protein; 8.5 g fat, 52% of calories (1 g saturated, 6% of calories; 4.9 g monounsaturated, 30%; 2.6 g polyunsaturated, 16%); 15 g carbohydrate; 4 g dietary fiber; 396 mg sodium; 0.9 mg iron; 0 mg cholesterol.

Thai Rice Salad

KHAO YUM

SERVES 4

1⅓ cups (11 fl oz/345 ml) water

⅔ cup (4 oz/125 g) jasmine or
   other long-grain rice

½ cup dried shrimp

¼ cup thinly sliced galangal
   or ginger

1 large grapefruit or pomelo,
   cut into segments

½ cup (2 oz/60 g) thinly sliced
   cucumber

2 stalks lemongrass, thinly sliced

6 lime leaves, thinly sliced

6 scallions (spring onions),
   thinly sliced

1 cup (2 oz/60 g) bean sprouts

2 tablespoons shredded mint

¼ cup (2 fl oz/60 ml) freshly
   squeezed lime juice

1 tablespoon fish sauce

1 tablespoon Thai sweet chili
   sauce

1 teaspoon superfine (caster) sugar

mint sprigs, for garnish

Cooked jasmine rice combined with refreshing ingredients like grapefruit and cucumber makes a sustaining salad or even a light meal. Add some freshly cooked shrimp for a treat. This recipe comes from southern Thailand.

PREPARATION   *30 minutes plus 1 hour cooling time*

✦ Place the water in a small saucepan and bring to a boil. Add the rice, stir well, then reduce the heat, cover and cook until tender, about 20 minutes. Transfer the rice to a bowl and let cool for 1 hour.

✦ Soak the dried shrimp in cold water for 10 minutes. Drain well, then chop finely in a food processor or blender.

ASSEMBLY   5 minutes

✦ Place the rice in a salad bowl. Add the shrimp, galangal, grapefruit, cucumber, lemongrass, lime leaves, scallions, bean sprouts and mint.

✦ Mix together the lime juice, fish sauce, chili sauce and sugar in a small bowl,.

✦ Just before serving, pour the lime dressing over the salad and toss well. Serve, garnished with the mint sprigs.

PER SERVING

206 calories/862 kilojoules; 12 g protein; 1.6 g fat, 7% of calories (0.03 g saturated, 0.1% of calories; 0.27 g monounsaturated, 1.2%; 1.3 g polyunsaturated, 5.7%); 35 g carbohydrate; 3 g dietary fiber; 215 mg sodium; 1.1 mg iron; 63 mg cholesterol.

Decorative brass rings are still used to elongate the neck among the hill tribes of northern Thailand.

Thai Rice Salad

Pasta Shells, Broccoli and Tomato Salad

In this recipe pasta shells and broccoli are partnered with colorful sun-dried tomatoes and cherry tomatoes, pungent goat cheese and a tangy citrus dressing. There are several forms of broccoli. The most commonly used is the dark green but try the purple or light green for a change.

SERVES 6

2½ cups (8 oz/250 g) small
   pasta shells
2 cups (5 oz/150 g) broccoli
   florets
¼ cup well-drained and thinly
   sliced sundried tomatoes
   packed in oil
½ cup halved cherry tomatoes
½ cup sliced, preserved artichoke
   hearts
2 oz (60 g) goat cheese or Feta
   cheese, cut into ½ in (1 cm)
   cubes
basil sprigs, for garnish

DRESSING

2 tablespoons extra virgin olive
   oil
¼ cup freshly squeezed orange
   juice
2 tablespoons tarragon-flavored
   white wine vinegar
1 garlic clove, crushed
3 tablespoons shredded basil
8 grinds black pepper

PREPARATION   *20 minutes*

◆ Bring a large pan of unsalted water to a boil. Add the pasta and boil rapidly, uncovered, until tender, about 10 minutes. Drain in a colander, rinse with cold water and set aside to cool.

◆ While the pasta is cooking, rinse the broccoli in cold water, then place in a clean, plastic bag. Twist the bag and fold under to seal, then place in a microwave oven and cook on High for 3 minutes or steam for 5 minutes. Remove and place immediately in a bowl of iced water to refresh the broccoli so that it retains its bright green color. Remove when cold.

◆ To make the dressing, place all of the ingredients in a glass jar. Cover tightly and shake until the dressing is well mixed. Refrigerate until required.

ASSEMBLY   *5 minutes*

◆ Place the pasta in a large mixing bowl. Add the broccoli, sun-dried tomatoes, cherry tomatoes and artichoke hearts.

◆ Shake the dressing and pour it over the pasta mixture. Toss well, using two plastic spoons, to avoid damaging the pasta.

◆ Place the salad in a serving bowl and sprinkle the goat cheese on top. Garnish with the basil sprigs and serve immediately.

PER SERVING

250 calories/1046 kilojoules; 9 g protein; 8.7 g fat, 32% of calories (2.6 g saturated, 9.9% of calories; 4.6 g monounsaturated, 17.3%; 1.5 g polyunsaturated, 4.8%); 34 g carbohydrate; 3.8 g dietary fiber; 176 mg sodium; 0.8 mg iron; 7 mg cholesterol.

*A weatherboard
Californian
home showing
the owner's
patriotism.*

*Pasta Shells, Broccoli
and Tomato Salad*

Rice with Spinach and Tomatoes
PALAK BHAATH

SERVES 6

2 cups (14 oz / 440 g) basmati
  or other long-grain rice
1 lb (500 g) spinach (English
  spinach), or 8 oz (250 g)
  frozen chopped spinach
2½ cups (20 fl oz / 600 ml) water
1 tablespoon vegetable oil
1 onion, thinly sliced
1 tablespoon mustard seeds
2 vine-ripened tomatoes, chopped
1 teaspoon ground coriander
2 teaspoons ground cumin
¼ teaspoon ground turmeric
¼ teaspoon salt

The central Indian state of Maharashtra is home to an established Jewish community. This recipe from Maharashtra is mildly flavored with curry spices and makes a versatile side dish that can be served with hot curries.

PREPARATION   *10 minutes plus 30 minutes soaking time*
✦ Wash the rice under cold running water until the water runs clear. Drain, then place it in a medium-sized bowl, cover with water and soak for 30 minutes.
✦ Wash and chop the spinach. Bring ½ cup (4 fl oz/ 125 ml) of the water to a boil over medium heat, add the spinach and cook until it wilts, then drain well, squeezing all the water out. (If using frozen spinach, thaw and drain well. Reduce the total water by ½ cup.)

COOKING   *50 minutes*
✦ Heat the oil in a large, heavy-bottomed saucepan over medium heat. Add the onion and mustard seeds and sauté, stirring occasionally, until the onion is golden, about 5 minutes.

✦ Drain the rice, add to the saucepan and cook, stirring continuously, for 2 minutes. Add the spinach, tomatoes, coriander, cumin, turmeric and salt and cook for 1 minute.
✦ Add the remaining water and bring to a boil, then cover and cook over low heat for 25 minutes. Remove the lid and stir the mixture well. Cover and continue cooking until the rice is tender, about 10 minutes.
✦ Spoon into a serving bowl.

PER SERVING
284 calories / 1189 kilojoules; 7 g protein; 3 g fat, 10% of calories (0.4 g saturated, 11% of calories; 0.6 g monounsaturated, 2%; 2 g polyunsaturated, 7%); 56 g carbohydrate; 5 g dietary fiber; 123 mg sodium; 3 mg iron; 0 mg cholesterol.

Saffron Rice
KESAY CHAAVAL

SERVES 6

½ teaspoon saffron threads
4 cups (32 fl oz / 1 l) boiling
  water
1½ cups (10½ oz / 330 g)
  basmati or other long-grain rice
2 tablespoons ghee
1 tablespoon black (dark)
  mustard seeds
1 large onion, finely chopped
2 teaspoons finely chopped ginger
3 cloves
1 cinnamon stick
1 teaspoon salt
⅓ cup (3 fl oz / 90 ml) freshly
  squeezed lime juice
2 tablespoons chopped cilantro
  (coriander) leaves
2 tablespoons shredded coconut
2 tablespoons roasted cashew nuts
1 red chili, thinly sliced
cilantro (coriander) sprigs,
  for garnish

Saffron threads, which are the stamens of the crocus flower, give saffron rice its lovely golden color. It takes 75,000 blossoms to make one pound (half a kilogram) of saffron! Use margarine instead of ghee to reduce the level of saturated fat.

PREPARATION   *10 minutes plus 10 minutes soaking time*
✦ In a small bowl, soak the saffron in 3 tablespoons of the boiling water for at least 10 minutes.
✦ Wash the rice under cold running water until the water runs clear. Drain.

COOKING   *40 minutes*
✦ Heat the ghee in a large, heavy-bottomed saucepan over medium heat. Add the mustard seeds, cover and cook, stirring frequently, until the seeds burst, about 2 to 3 minutes. Add the onion, ginger, cloves and cinnamon stick, reduce the heat to low and cook, stirring occasionally, until the onion is golden, about 5 minutes.
✦ Add the rice and cook over medium heat, stirring, for 3 minutes. Add the remaining boiling water and

the salt and bring to a boil over high heat, stirring continuously. Add the lime juice, cilantro, coconut and the saffron and its liquid, stir well and reduce the heat to low. Cover and cook until the rice is tender and has absorbed all of the liquid, about 25 minutes,.
✦ Stir the rice with a fork and sprinkle with the cashew nuts and red chili. Transfer to a serving dish, garnish with the cilantro and serve.

PER SERVING
262 calories / 1095 kilojoules; 5 g protein; 8 g fat, 26% of calories (4 g saturated, 14% of calories; 3 g monounsaturated, 10%; 1 g polyunsaturated, 2%); 43 g carbohydrate; 3 g dietary fiber; 344 mg sodium; 1 mg iron; 11 mg cholesterol.

Saffron Rice (top) and Rice with Spinach and Tomatoes

Bhopali Pilaf with Fresh Peas
BHOPALI MATAR PILAO

SERVES 4

*2 cups (14 oz/440 g) basmati
　or other long-grain rice*
2½ in (5 cm) ginger, chopped
6 garlic cloves, crushed
*2½ cups (20 fl oz/600 ml)
　water*
*2 tablespoons vegetable oil
　or ghee*
4 cloves
3 cardamom pods
1 cinnamon stick
¼ teaspoon cumin seeds
2 curry leaves or bay leaves
1 onion, thinly sliced
¼ teaspoon salt
*1 cup (5 oz/150 g) shelled
　green peas*
½ cup halved cherry tomatoes

Bhopal, the capital of Madhya Pradesh is a charming old city where Muslim influence is evident in the local cuisine. This aromatic rice dish is a perfect accompaniment to lamb curries.

PREPARATION　　*15 minutes plus 30 minutes soaking time*
◆ Wash the rice under cold running water until the water runs clear. Drain, then place it in a medium-sized bowl, cover with water and soak for 30 minutes.

COOKING　　　　　　　　　　　*40 minutes*
◆ Place the ginger, garlic and 1 tablespoon of the water in a blender and blend to a paste.
◆ Heat the oil in a large, heavy-bottomed saucepan over medium heat. Add the cloves, cardamom, cinnamon, cumin seeds and curry leaves and stir for 1 minute.
◆ Add the onion and cook, stirring continuously, until golden, for 5 minutes. Add the ginger mixture and cook, stirring continuously, for 2 minutes.

◆ Drain the rice and add to the saucepan. Reduce the heat to low and cook, stirring continuously, for 3 minutes. Add the remaining water and the salt and bring to a boil.
◆ Add the peas and tomatoes, cover, reduce the heat to low and cook until the rice is tender and all the water has been absorbed, about 25 minutes. Stir well.
◆ Spoon into a serving bowl and serve.

PER SERVING
484 calories/2028 kilojoules; 10 g protein; 8 g fat, 15% of calories (0.9 g saturated, 1.6% of calories; 1.4 g monounsaturated, 2.7%; 5.7 g polyunsaturated, 10.7%); 92 g carbohydrate; 6.1 g dietary fiber; 110 mg sodium; 1.7 mg iron; 0 mg cholesterol.

Rice with Potatoes, Cilantro and Mint
HARI CHATNI PILAO

SERVES 6

½ teaspoon saffron threads
*1½ cups (12 fl oz/375 ml)
　boiling water*
*2 cups (14 oz/440 g) basmati
　or other long-grain rice*
2 tablespoons vegetable oil
4 cloves
1 cinnamon stick
*2 potatoes (about 8 oz/250 g),
　cut into ½ in (1 cm) cubes*
2 tablespoons chopped mint
*1 tablespoon finely chopped
　ginger*
*½ cup (4 oz/125 g) low-fat
　plain yogurt*
¼ teaspoon salt
*¼ cup chopped cilantro
　(coriander)*
1 onion, thinly sliced

This dish is served at religious celebrations in the north of India. It is also a sustaining, cold weather dish in the mountain regions. It makes a delicious accompaniment for chicken or meat curries.

PREPARATION　　　　　　　　*20 minutes*
◆ Soak the saffron in a small bowl in 1 tablespoon of the boiling water for at least 10 minutes.
◆ Wash the rice under cold running water until the water runs clear. Drain, then place it in a medium-sized bowl, cover with water and soak for 30 minutes.
◆ Preheat the oven to 350°F (180°C).

COOKING　　　　　　　　　　*25 minutes*
◆ Bring a large saucepan of water to a boil. Add the rice, stir well, and boil rapidly for 5 minutes. Drain.
◆ While the rice is cooking, heat the oil in a large, flameproof casserole dish over medium heat. Add the cloves and cinnamon and stir for 30 seconds. Add the potatoes and cook, stirring frequently, until golden, about 5 minutes. Remove from the heat. Sprinkle the mint and half of the ginger over the potato mixture.
◆ Spread half of the rice over the potato mixture.
◆ Place the yogurt, salt, saffron and saffron liquid in a

small bowl. Combine well. Pour half of the yogurt mixture over the rice in the casserole dish.
◆ Sprinkle the remaining ginger, the cilantro and onion on top and cover with the remaining rice. Pour the remaining yogurt mixture over the rice.
◆ Pour the remaining boiling water down the side of the mixture. Cover and bake in the oven until the rice is tender and all of the liquid is absorbed, about 15 minutes.
◆ Loosen the edges of the mixture from the casserole dish with a knife. Turn the rice mixture out onto a warm serving platter. Serve immediately.

PER SERVING
340 calories/1423 kilojoules; 7 g protein; 5.2 g fat, 14% of calories (0.6 g saturated, 1.7% of calories; 0.9 g monounsaturated, 2.4%; 3.7 g polyunsaturated, 9.9%); 65 g carbohydrate; 2.4 g dietary fiber; 91 mg sodium; 0.8 mg iron; 0.4 mg cholesterol.

*Rice with Potatoes, Cilantro and Mint and
Bhopali Pilaf with Fresh Peas (top)*

Hyderabadi Pilaf
HYDERABADI PILAO

SERVES 6

½ cup (2 oz/60 g) chana dal
2 cups (14 oz/440 g) basmati
   or other long-grain rice
½ teaspoon ground saffron
6 cups (48 fl oz/1.5 l) water
1 tablespoon vegetable oil
1 large onion, thinly sliced
1 garlic clove, crushed
2 teaspoons finely chopped ginger
1 cup (8 oz/250 g) low-fat
   plain yogurt
1 carrot, grated
¼ cup (1½ oz/45 g) raisins
2 teaspoons garam masala
2 tablespoons lemon juice
2 green chilies, finely chopped
¼ cup chopped cilantro (coriander)

SAUCE (OPTIONAL)

1 cup (8 oz/250 g) low-fat
   plain yogurt
¼ cup (2 fl oz/60 ml) extra
   virgin olive oil
2 teaspoons honey
1 tablespoon lemon juice
¼ cup chopped mint

Hyderabad has preserved the cuisine of its once wealthy Muslim court. *Chana dal* is a type of yellow split pea; if unavailable, substitute yellow split peas. For a vegetarian meal, serve this pilaf with the optional sauce and a green salad.

PREPARATION   *15 minutes plus 1½ hours soaking time*
♦ Place the chana dal in a medium-sized bowl, cover with cold water by 3 in (8 cm) and soak for 1½ hours.
♦ Wash the rice under cold running water until the water runs clear. Drain, then place it in a medium-sized bowl, cover with water and soak for 30 minutes.

COOKING   *1 hour and 5 minutes*
♦ Place the chana dal with its soaking liquid in a medium-sized saucepan. Add half of the saffron, cover and bring to a boil. Reduce the heat and simmer until tender, about 30 minutes. Drain.
♦ Meanwhile, bring the 6 cups of water to a boil in a large saucepan. Drain the rice, add to the saucepan and boil rapidly, uncovered, for 5 minutes. Drain.
♦ Preheat the oven to 350°F (180°C).
♦ Heat the oil in a medium-sized, non-stick skillet over medium heat. Add the onion and cook, stirring occasionally, until golden brown, about 5 minutes.

Using a slotted spoon, transfer the onion to a plate lined with paper towels to drain.
♦ Add the garlic, ginger and the remaining saffron to the skillet. Stir for 1 minute. Add the yogurt, carrot, raisins, garam masala and chana dal and stir.
♦ Place half the rice in a large baking dish. Cover with the chana dal mixture, then top with the remaining rice. Sprinkle with the onions, lemon juice, chilies and cilantro. Cover the dish with aluminum foil and bake until hot, about 30 minutes. Stir well before serving.
♦ If using the sauce, mix all of the ingredients together and serve in a separate bowl.

PER SERVING (THIS INCLUDES THE SAUCE)
459 calories/1922 kilojoules; 14 g protein; 13 g fat, 25% of calories (2.1 g saturated, 4% of calories; 7.7 g monounsaturated, 14.7%; 3.2 g polyunsaturated, 6.3%); 71 g carbohydrate; 3.4 g dietary fiber; 89 mg sodium; 1.2 mg iron; 1.7 mg cholesterol.

Yogurt Rice
MASURA ANNA BANGALORE

SERVES 6

1 cup (7 oz/220 g) basmati or
   other long-grain rice
1 cup (8 oz/250 g) low-fat
   plain yogurt
½ teaspoon salt
1 tablespoon vegetable oil
½ teaspoon black mustard seeds
½ teaspoon urad dal or white
   split peas, optional
8 fresh or dried curry leaves
2 dried red chilies
2 green chilies, very finely
   chopped
2 teaspoons finely chopped ginger
1 tablespoon chopped cilantro
   (coriander)

This is a popular travelers' snack and may be bought at most railway stations in southern India. It is usually served at room temperature. The yogurt makes a cool contrast to the heat of the spices.

PREPARATION   *5 minutes plus 30 minutes soaking time*
♦ Wash the rice under cold running water until the water runs clear. Drain and then place it in a medium-sized bowl, cover with water and soak for 30 minutes.

COOKING   *20 minutes*
♦ Place the yogurt and salt in a large mixing bowl and beat with a fork until smooth.
♦ Bring a large, heavy-bottomed saucepan of water to a boil. Drain the rice, add to the saucepan and boil rapidly until tender, about 10 to 12 minutes. Drain, add to the yogurt while still hot and combine well.
♦ Heat the oil in a small skillet over medium heat. Add the mustard seeds and stir until they start to burst,

about 2 to 3 minutes. Add the urad dal, if using, and stir until it turns red. Add the curry leaves and red chilies and stir for 30 seconds.
♦ Remove the mustard seed mixture from the heat and pour over the rice. Add the green chilies, ginger and cilantro. Toss gently to combine well.
♦ Transfer to a serving dish and serve immediately.

PER SERVING
178 calories/745 kilojoules; 6 g protein; 2.7 g fat, 14% of calories (0.4 g saturated, 2.1% of calories; 0.5 g monounsaturated, 2.7%; 1.8 g polyunsaturated, 9.2%); 32 g carbohydrate; 1.1 g dietary fiber; 206 mg sodium; 0.4 mg iron; 1 mg cholesterol.

Hyderabadi Pilaf

Couscous Marrakech with Lemon
COUSCOUS MARRAKCHY B'LHAMAD

SERVES 4

1⅓ cups (8 oz/250 g) precooked
    couscous
1 cup (8 fl oz/250 ml)
    vegetable stock
1 tablespoon virgin olive oil
1 tablespoon unsalted butter
1 garlic clove, crushed
½ cup thinly sliced scallions
    (spring onions)
¼ cup (2 fl oz/60 ml) freshly
    squeezed lemon juice
3 tablespoons well-drained, diced
    pickled lemon, optional
4 fresh dates, seeded and cut
    in strips
¼ cup (4 oz/125 g) pistachio
    nuts, halved
2 tablespoons snipped chives
extra pickled lemon wedges,
    or fresh lemon, for garnish

Couscous is usually served with stews in North Africa, but with a little imagination, you can also prepare it as a tasty, light side dish. This version makes a delicious accompaniment to broiled or barbecued fish or roast chicken.

PREPARATION   20 minutes
✦ Place the couscous in a medium-sized bowl. Bring the stock to a boil in a small saucepan and pour it over the couscous. Stir well, then let the couscous stand for 5 minutes to swell, stirring occasionally to separate the grains as they absorb the water.

COOKING   10 minutes
✦ Heat the oil and butter in a large, heavy-bottomed saucepan over medium heat. Add the garlic and cook gently for 1 minute.
✦ Stir the couscous with a fork, then add to the saucepan together with the scallions and lemon juice. Cook gently over low heat, stirring continuously, until hot, about 4 minutes. Remove from the heat.

✦ Add the pickled lemon, if using, and the dates, pistachios and chives and stir gently until combined.
✦ Spoon onto a serving platter and serve, garnished with the wedges of pickled or fresh lemon.

PER SERVING
225 calories/1066 kilojoules; 5 g protein; 10 g fat, 36% of calories (2.9 g saturated, 10.4% of calories; 5.4 g monounsaturated, 19.5%; 1.7 g polyunsaturated, 6.1%); 37 g carbohydrate; 2.3 g dietary fiber; 8 mg sodium; 3.6 mg iron; 8.6 mg cholesterol.

Moroccan Sheikh's Couscous
SHEIKH'S COUSCOUS MAROCAINE

SERVES 4

1⅓ cups (8 oz/250 g) precooked
    couscous
1⅓ cups (11 fl oz/340 ml)
    boiling water
1½ cups (12 fl oz/375 ml)
    vegetable or chicken stock,
    skimmed of fat
3 tablespoons butter
½ cup (3¼ oz/100 g) cooked
    chickpeas
½ cup (2½ oz/80 g) raisins
finely grated zest and juice of
    1 orange
2 tablespoons chopped parsley

This is a delicious side dish to accompany Middle Eastern-style stuffed vegetables. It also complements roast dishes as well as chicken or lamb stews. Most of the packaged couscous sold today is presteamed so it cooks quickly.

PREPARATION   10 minutes
✦ Place the couscous in a shallow dish and add the boiling water. Stir well, then let the couscous stand for 5 minutes to swell, stirring occasionally to separate the grains as they absorb the water.

COOKING   10 minutes
✦ Place the stock in a large, heavy-bottomed saucepan and bring to a boil over medium-high heat. Add the couscous, butter, chickpeas and raisins, reduce the heat and simmer, stirring continuously with a fork, for 5 minutes.

✦ Add the orange zest and juice and half of the chopped parsley. Stir well to combine and heat through, about 1 minute.
✦ Transfer to a serving platter and serve hot, sprinkled with the remaining parsley.

PER SERVING
323 calories/1352 kilojoules; 7 g protein; 11 g fat, 29% of calories (6.8 g saturated, 18% of calories; 3 g monounsaturated, 7.8%; 1.2 g polyunsaturated, 3.2%); 53 g carbohydrate; 2.9 g dietary fiber; 287 mg sodium; 4.7 mg iron; 23 mg cholesterol.

Couscous Marrakech with Lemon (top)
and Moroccan Sheikh's Couscous

Kasha and Vegetable Ring

KASHA S OVSHNIE KOLTSA

Buckwheat, combined with unusual winter vegetables, gives a nutty taste and texture to this nourishing dish. It is a delicious accompaniment for meatballs or grilled fish, or can be served with a spinach salad to make a light vegetarian meal.

SERVES 6

1 tablespoon vegetable oil
¾ cup (5 oz/150 g) kasha
   (buckwheat groats)
2½ cups (20 fl oz/600 ml)
   boiling water
8 oz (250 g) leeks, diced
8 oz (250 g) celeriac or celery,
   diced
8 oz (250 g) Jerusalem
   artichokes, scrubbed and diced
8 oz (250 g) mushrooms,
   chopped
2 garlic cloves, crushed
2 tablespoons white wine vinegar
2 teaspoons paprika
1 tablespoon toasted sesame seeds
¼ teaspoon salt
¼ teaspoon freshly ground white
   pepper
1 cup (8 oz/250 g) low-fat,
   plain yogurt or sour cream
1 teaspoon prepared horseradish
1 tablespoon capers
chopped chives, for garnish

PREPARATION   *30 minutes*
✦ Line the bottom of a 6-cup ring mold with a circle of non-stick baking paper, and grease the sides of the mold lightly.
✦ Preheat the oven to 350°F (180°C).

COOKING   *50 minutes*
✦ Heat 1 teaspoon of the oil in a medium-sized saucepan over medium heat. Add the kasha and cook, stirring continuously, for 4 minutes. Add the boiling water. Cover and simmer over low heat until tender, about 20 minutes. Drain.
✦ Heat the remaining oil in a large, heavy-bottomed saucepan over low heat. Add the leeks, celeriac, artichokes, mushrooms and garlic, cover and cook, shaking the saucepan frequently, for 10 minutes.
✦ Add the kasha, vinegar, paprika, sesame seeds, salt and pepper, and mix well.

✦ Place the mixture in the prepared mold and press down evenly. Cover with aluminum foil. Bake for 40 minutes.
✦ Meanwhile, mix together the yogurt, horseradish and capers in a small serving bowl. Refrigerate until ready to serve.
✦ Turn the ring out onto a warm plate. Garnish the yogurt mixture with the chives and serve with the kasha and vegetable ring.

PER SERVING
163 calories/684 kilojoules; 7 g protein; 4 g fat, 24% of calories (0.6 g saturated, 3.6% of calories; 0.9 g monounsaturated, 5.5%; 2.5 g polyunsaturated, 14.9%); 21 g carbohydrate; 8.2 g dietary fiber; 88 mg sodium; 2.2 mg iron; 0 mg cholesterol.

Kasha with Mushrooms

KASHA S GRIBAMI

In Russian "kasha" refers to buckwheat and some other types of grains. In English "kasha" designates only the cracked kernels of buckwheat. This dish is traditionally served with roast pork but also complements broiled or barbecued fish or chicken.

SERVES 4

1 cup (5½ oz/175 g) kasha
   (buckwheat groats)
4 cups (32 fl oz/1 l) reduced-
   sodium chicken stock,
   skimmed of fat, plus extra
   if required
2 oz (60 g) butter
1 onion, finely chopped
8 oz (250 g) mushrooms, finely
   chopped
3 tablespoons chopped parsley
finely grated zest and juice of
   1 lemon

PREPARATION   *15 minutes*
✦ Wash the kasha under cold running water until the water runs clear. Drain well.

COOKING   *35 minutes*
✦ Pour the stock into a large saucepan, cover and bring to a boil. Add the kasha and boil, half-covered, until tender, about 20 minutes. Drain off the stock that has not been absorbed. Cover the cooked kasha to keep warm.
✦ In another large saucepan melt the butter over low heat. Add the onion and cook, stirring occasionally, for 5 minutes. Add the mushrooms and cook, stirring occasionally, for 4 minutes.

✦ Add the kasha, parsley and lemon zest and juice. Combine well until heated through. If the kasha is too dry, stir in a little extra chicken stock and warm through gently.
✦ Transfer to a serving dish and serve hot.

PER SERVING
262 calories/1095 kilojoules; 9 g protein; 9.6 g fat, 36% of calories (6.1 g saturated, 23% of calories; 2.9 g monounsaturated, 10.8%; 0.6 g polyunsaturated, 2.2%); 30 g carbohydrate; 7.9 g dietary fiber; 392 mg sodium; 3 mg iron; 65 mg cholesterol.

Kasha and Vegetable Ring

Spanish Saffron Rice
ARROZ CON AZAFRAN ESPANOL

VALENCIA

Gulf of
Valencia

Valencia

SERVES 4

1¼ cups (8½ oz/275 g) long-
  grain rice
2 large red bell peppers
  (capsicums)
1 tablespoon virgin olive oil
1 small onion, finely chopped
2½ cups (20 fl oz/600 ml)
  vegetable stock
generous pinch crushed saffron
  threads
generous pinch salt
2 vine-ripened tomatoes
2 teaspoons extra virgin olive oil
1 tablespoon lemon juice
freshly ground black pepper,
  to taste
8 black olives, pitted cut into
  strips, for garnish
flat-leaf parsley, for garnish

The Levante region, on the east coast of Spain, is not only the "Land of Rice," but the region where purple beds of crocuses flourish. Their orange stigmas are prized for the expensive spice called saffron. Serve this dish with grilled fish or chicken.

PREPARATION   *10 minutes*

◆ Wash the rice under cold running water until the water runs clear. Drain.
◆ Preheat a broiler (grill).
◆ Cut the peppers into segments, following the natural indentations, and remove the seeds and white membrane. Place the pepper segments, skin upwards, under the broiler. Cook until the skin bubbles and starts to char. Place the peppers in a clean, plastic bag, seal and cover with a cloth in order to create steam in the bag. Leave for 5 minutes. Remove the peppers from the bag and carefully rub off the skin. Keep warm or reheat in a microwave oven when needed.

COOKING   *30 minutes*

◆ Heat the tablespoon of oil in a large, heavy-bottomed saucepan over low heat. Add the onion and cook, stirring occasionally, until soft, about 3 minutes.
◆ Meanwhile, bring the vegetable stock to a boil in a separate saucepan.

◆ Add the rice to the saucepan with the onion and stir for 3 minutes. Add the boiling stock, saffron and salt. Increase the heat and bring to a boil, stirring continuously. Cover the saucepan, reduce the heat to low and cook until the rice is tender and all of the liquid has been absorbed, about 20 minutes. Stir the rice with a fork.
◆ While the rice is cooking, prepare the tomatoes by cutting each one horizontally into 4 thick slices. Place a sheet of aluminum foil on the broiler rack, place the tomato slices on the foil and cook until hot and the flesh has softened.
◆ Mix the 2 teaspoons of oil with the lemon juice.
◆ To serve, arrange the saffron rice on a warm serving platter. Place the bell peppers and tomatoes on the center of the rice, grind the pepper on top and drizzle with the oil and lemon juice mixture.
◆ Serve, garnished with the olive strips and parsley.

PER SERVING
307 calories/1285 kilojoules; 6 g protein; 6.5 g fat, 19% of calories (1 g saturated, 2.9% of calories; 4.6 g monounsaturated, 13.5%; 0.9 g polyunsaturated, 2.6%); 55 g carbohydrate; 3.3 g dietary fiber; 78 mg sodium; 0.9 mg iron; 0 mg cholesterol.

A balcony is a good place to enjoy the atmosphere on Ibiza, one of the Balearic Islands.

Coconut Rice

KHAO MAN

SERVES 4

1¼ cups (12½ oz/350 g)
 jasmine or other long-grain rice
2 in (5 cm) lemongrass
5 teaspoons vegetable oil
¾ cup (6 fl oz/180 ml) coconut
 milk
¾ cup (6 fl oz/180 ml) water
pinch of salt, optional
3 dried kaffir lime or lime leaves
½ cup (1½ oz/45 g) toasted
 shredded coconut, optional
½ cup shredded purple basil or
 cilantro (coriander), optional
4 scallions (spring onions),
 diagonally sliced, optional
purple basil or cilantro
 (coriander) leaves, for garnish

Use a saucepan with a thick bottom to prepare this dish. A thin crust of rice is likely to form on the bottom of the pan, and the thicker the pan bottom, the less likely the rice is to burn. Kaffir lime leaves are available from Asian food stores.

PREPARATION   *10 minutes plus 1 hour soaking time*

◆ Soak the rice in a bowl of cold water for 1 hour. Drain, wash under cold running water until the water runs clear. Drain again.
◆ Crush the lemongrass with the flat side of a cleaver.

COOKING   *40 minutes*

◆ Heat the oil in a medium-sized, heavy-bottomed saucepan over medium heat. Add the rice and cook, stirring frequently, for 3 minutes.
◆ Add the coconut milk, water, lemongrass, salt and kaffir lime leaves. Bring to a boil, then reduce the heat and simmer until the rice has absorbed all of the liquid, about 10 minutes. Stir frequently to prevent the rice from sticking to the bottom of the saucepan.

◆ Cover, reduce the heat to low and cook until the rice is tender, about 12 to 15 minutes. Remove the lemongrass and kaffir lime leaves and discard.
◆ Stir the coconut, basil and scallions, if using, into the hot rice, scraping any crust from the bottom of the saucepan.
◆ Transfer to a serving dish. Serve, garnished with the purple basil or cilantro leaves.

PER SERVING
497 calories/2081 kilojoules; 8 g protein; 19 g fat, 35% of calories (12.2 g saturated, 22.4% of calories; 1.9 g monounsaturated, 3.5%; 4.9 g polyunsaturated, 9.1%); 73 g carbohydrate; 4.1 g dietary fiber; 41 mg sodium; 1.6 mg iron; 0 mg cholesterol.

Bonsai trees enhance the regal court-yard of the magnificent Grand Palace in Bangkok.

Wild Rice Pilaf

Wild rice is not really rice at all; it is a high-protein aquatic grass seed that is native to the northern United States and southern Canada. Serve this pilaf with roast turkey or chicken, or sprinkle with Parmesan cheese and serve with a salad for a vegetarian meal.

PREPARATION   *15 minutes*

✦ Preheat the broiler (grill).
✦ Wash the rice under cold running water until the water runs clear. Drain.
✦ Toast the almonds under the broiler until golden, about 2 to 3 minutes, or in a moderate oven for 5 to 10 minutes.

COOKING   *1 hour*

✦ Bring the stock to a boil in a large, heavy-bottomed saucepan over medium heat. Add the rice, stir well, then reduce the heat, cover the saucepan and simmer until the rice splits open, about 45 to 50 minutes. Drain, transfer to a medium-sized bowl and keep warm.
✦ Melt the butter in a large, heavy-bottomed saucepan over medium heat. Add the scallions and cook,

stirring continuously, for about 1 minute.
✦ Add the mushrooms and cook, stirring frequently, until they change color, about 1 minute.
✦ Add the rice, tomatoes, almonds and shredded mint and stir until the rice grains are evenly coated with butter and heated through.
✦ Place on a serving platter and serve hot, garnished with the mint sprigs.

PER SERVING

360 calories/1509 kilojoules; 11 g protein; 18 g fat, 47% of calories (2.8 g saturated, 7.2% of calories; 8.1 g monounsaturated, 21.4%; 7.1 g polyunsaturated, 18.4%); 39 g carbohydrate; 3.9 g dietary fiber; 144 mg sodium; 1.5 mg iron; 0 mg cholesterol.

Brown Rice Pilaf

Brown rice is high in fiber because its bran layer is still intact (to make white rice, the bran is removed.) The outer layer imparts a nutty flavor and gives the grain a chewy texture. It is tasty and also easy to cook, taking only a little more time than white rice.

PREPARATION   *15 minutes*

✦ Preheat the broiler (grill).
✦ Toast the cashews under a broiler (grill) until golden, about 2 to 3 minutes, or in a moderate oven for 5 to 10 minutes.
✦ Peel two of the oranges, removing all of the white pith, and divide the flesh into segments. Squeeze the remaining orange and reserve the juice.

COOKING   *45 minutes*

✦ Bring a large saucepan of water to a boil. Add the rice and cook, uncovered, until tender, about 40 minutes. Drain, rinse under hot, running water, then drain again. Cover to keep warm.
✦ Melt the butter in a large, heavy-bottomed skillet over low heat. Add the onion and garlic and cook, stirring frequently, for 5 minutes.

✦ Add the five-spice powder and cook, stirring, for 30 seconds, then add the celery and the cilantro root and cook, stirring, for 1 minute. Add the orange juice and rice and stir over low heat until the rice is heated through.
✦ Gently stir in the cilantro leaves and orange segments.
✦ Sprinkle with the cashews and serve hot.

PER SERVING

416 calories/1741 kilojoules; 8 g protein; 12.7 g fat, 34% of calories (2.5 g saturated, 6.5% of calories; 6 g monounsaturated, 17%; 4.2 g polyunsaturated, 10.5%); 60 g carbohydrate; 5.9 g dietary fiber; 129 mg sodium; 2 mg iron; 0 mg cholesterol.

Brown Rice Pilaf (left) and Wild Rice Pilaf

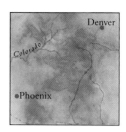

Quinoa with Spring Greens

SERVES 4

1 cup baby spinach (English spinach)
1 cup romaine (cos) lettuce
1 cup arugula (rocket)
1 cup (6 oz / 180 g) quinoa
1 tablespoon virgin olive oil
8 scallions (spring onions), thinly sliced diagonally
finely grated zest of 1 lemon
1 tablespoon freshly squeezed lemon juice
1 tablespoon chili sauce
½ teaspoon brown sugar

Quinoa is a rice-like grain from the plant of the same name. It is pronounced "keenwa" and is available in specialty food stores. When cooked, it has a delicate, light texture and flavor. Here it is used to make an unusual side dish to accompany roasted meat or barbecued fish.

PREPARATION   *10 minutes*

✦ Wash, pat dry and shred the spinach, romaine lettuce and arugula leaves. Keep the arugula leaves separate from the spinach and romaine lettuce.

COOKING   *10 to 12 minutes*

✦ Cook the quinoa according to the package directions. Drain well and keep warm.
✦ Heat the oil in a non-stick skillet over medium heat. Add the scallions and cook, stirring continuously, for 2 minutes. Add the spinach and romaine lettuce and cook for 1 minute.

✦ Reduce the heat to low. Add the lemon zest, lemon juice, chili sauce, sugar and quinoa and toss until well combined. Cover and cook until heated through, about 1 minute.
✦ Add the arugula and toss well. Transfer to a serving dish and serve immediately.

PER SERVING

230 calories / 962 kilojoules; 8 g protein; 3.4 g fat, 28% of calories (0.5 g saturated, 4.2% of calories; 2.6 g monounsaturated, 21%; 0.3 g polyunsaturated, 2.8%); 34 g carbohydrate; 5.9 g dietary fiber; 37 mg sodium; 0.6 mg iron; 0 mg cholesterol.

The two pinnacles of rock are the instantly recognizable features of Monument Valley, Arizona.

Spicy Rice

NASI KUNING

Rice is a staple of the Indonesian diet, and it is cooked in many different ways. This is a bright yellow rice dish which is traditionally served at celebration meals in Java. It may be served with fish or meat dishes.

SERVES 4

1½ cups (10½ oz / 330 g)
    jasmine or other long-grain
    rice
2 tablespoons vegetable oil
1 teaspoon ground turmeric
1 teaspoon ground coriander
½ teaspoon ground cumin
½ teaspoon ground nutmeg
¾ cup (6 fl oz / 180 ml) coconut
    milk
¾ cup (6 fl oz / 180 ml) reduced-
    sodium chicken stock,
    skimmed of fat
1 cinnamon stick
2 cloves
1 salam leaf or bay leaf
cilantro (coriander) leaves, for
    garnish

PREPARATION   *10 minutes plus 1 hour soaking time*
◆ Soak the rice in cold water for 1 hour. Drain, wash under cold running water until the water runs clear. Drain again.

COOKING   *25 minutes*
◆ Heat the oil in a medium-sized, heavy-bottomed saucepan over medium heat. Add the rice and cook, stirring continuously, about 2 minutes.
◆ Add the turmeric, coriander, cumin and nutmeg and cook for 2 minutes.
◆ Add the coconut milk, stock, cinnamon, cloves and salam leaf. Bring to a boil, then reduce the heat to low and simmer until all of the liquid has been absorbed, about 10 minutes.

◆ Cover, reduce the heat to very low and cook until the rice is tender, about 10 minutes. Alternatively, transfer the rice mixture to a steamer and steam over simmering water for 10 minutes.
◆ Remove the salam leaf and discard. Spoon the rice onto a serving platter and serve, garnished with the cilantro.

PER SERVING
425 calories / 1780 kilojoules; 6 g protein; 14 g fat, 30% of calories (6.9 g saturated, 14.7% of calories; 1.6 g monounsaturated, 3.6%; 5.5 g polyunsaturated, 11.7%); 68 g carbohydrate; 1.9 g dietary fiber; 155 mg sodium; 0.6 mg iron; 0 mg cholesterol.

The graceful posture of a local woman as she carries produce, Bali-style.

Rice with Mango

NASI MANGGA

SERVES 4

2 cups (14 oz/440 g) jasmine
    or other long-grain rice
6 scallions (spring onions)
2 tablespoons peanut oil
2 large green chilies, seeded and
    thinly sliced
2 garlic cloves, crushed
2 teaspoons reduced-sodium
    soy sauce
2 teaspoons fish sauce
2 tablespoons freshly squeezed
    lime juice
1 large mango, peeled, seeded
    and thinly sliced
3 tablespoons chopped candlenuts
2 tablespoons chopped cilantro
    (coriander)

Mango and candlenuts give this version of Indonesian fried rice a unique flavor. It is a delicious base for satay. Candlenuts are available at Asian food stores; substitute macadamia nuts if you prefer.

PREPARATION   *20 minutes*

✦ Wash the rice under cold running water until the water runs clear. Drain well. Bring a large saucepan of water to a boil. Add the rice and boil for 10 minutes. Drain again.
✦ Thinly slice the scallions diagonally, keeping the green parts separate from the white parts.

COOKING   *8 minutes*

✦ Heat the oil in a wok or large, heavy-bottomed skillet over medium heat. Add the chilies, the white part of the scallions and the garlic and cook, stirring continuously, for 1 minute.
✦ Add the rice and cook, stirring occasionally, until the rice is hot, about 5 minutes.

✦ Add the soy sauce, fish sauce, lime juice, mango, candlenuts, the green part of the scallions and half the cilantro. Cook, stirring continuously, for 2 minutes.
✦ Transfer to a serving platter. Sprinkle the remaining cilantro on top and serve immediately.

PER SERVING

548 calories/2295 kilojoules; 11 g protein; 14 g fat, 23% of calories (2.7 g saturated, 4.4% of calories; 5.7 g monounsaturated, 9.4%; 5.6 g polyunsaturated, 9.2%); 95 g carbohydrate; 4.3 g dietary fiber; 134 mg sodium; 1.5 mg iron; 0 mg cholesterol.

Fragrant Rice

NASI MINYAK

SERVES 4

1 large onion
2 garlic cloves
1 tablespoon peanut oil
1 teaspoon ground turmeric
½ teaspoon five-spice powder
2 tablespoons sliced almonds
1 cup (7 oz/220 g) jasmine or
    other long-grain rice
2 kaffir lime leaves or
    lime leaves
1½ cups (12 fl oz/375 ml)
    water
cilantro (coriander) or parsley,
    for garnish, optional

Indonesian cooks are famous for their handling of spices. This is not surprising given the abundance of spices that grow on many of the islands, including the Moluccas, once known as the Spice Islands. Serve this with your favorite curry.

PREPARATION   *5 minutes*

✦ Thinly slice the onion and crush the garlic.

COOKING   *30 to 40 minutes*

✦ Heat the oil in a large, heavy-bottomed saucepan over medium heat. Add the onion and garlic and cook, stirring frequently, for 5 minutes.
✦ Add the turmeric, five-spice powder and 1 tablespoon of the almonds, and cook, stirring continuously, for 1 minute.
✦ Add the rice and kaffir lime leaves and cook, stirring continuously, for 2 minutes.
✦ Add the water and bring to a boil, stirring frequently. Reduce the heat to low, cover and cook until the rice is tender and all of the liquid has been absorbed, 25 to 30 minutes.

✦ Remove the rice from the heat and stir with a fork.
✦ Spoon the rice into a warm serving bowl, sprinkle with the remaining almonds and garnish with the cilantro, if using. Serve.

PER SERVING

269 calories/1125 kilojoules; 5 g protein; 7.3 g fat, 25% of calories (1 g saturated, 3.4% of calories; 4 g monounsaturated, 13.7%; 2.3 g polyunsaturated, 7.9%); 45 g carbohydrate; 2.5 g dietary fiber; 8 mg sodium; 0.8 mg iron; 0 mg cholesterol.

Fragrant Rice (top) and Rice with Mango

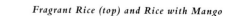

Chicken, Vegetable and Noodle Stir-Fry

JIRU QING CAI CHAO MIEN

SERVES 4

8 oz (250 g) fresh egg noodles
2 chicken breast fillets, about
    4 oz (125 g) each
2 tablespoons peanut or corn oil
2 onions, each cut into 12 wedges
1 garlic clove, crushed
½ teaspoon finely chopped ginger
½ teaspoon finely chopped red chili
2 carrots, thinly sliced diagonally
2 cups shredded spinach or
    Chinese broccoli
½ teaspoon sesame oil
2 tablespoons oyster sauce
2 tablespoons plum sauce
2 tablespoons sake (rice wine)
    or mirin (sweet rice wine)
½ cup (4 fl oz / 125 ml) reduced-
    sodium chicken stock,
    skimmed of fat
1 cup (2 oz / 60 g) bean sprouts
½ cup (1 oz / 30 g) snow pea
    (mange-tout) sprouts

The Chinese developed stir-frying out of necessity to conserve fuel. Today it is recognized as a low-fat, quick and healthy cooking method that also conserves nutrients, textures and flavors.

PREPARATION   *30 minutes*

✦ Bring a large saucepan of water to a boil. Add the noodles and cook, stirring occasionally, until just tender, about 5 minutes. Drain.
✦ Cut the chicken into thin strips.

COOKING   *15 minutes*

✦ Heat the peanut oil in a wok or large, non-stick skillet over medium-high heat. Add the chicken and stir-fry until the chicken strips are golden, about 2 minutes. Using a slotted spoon, transfer the chicken to a plate. Cover to keep warm.
✦ Add the onion, garlic, ginger and chili to the wok and stir-fry for 1 minute.
✦ Add the carrot and stir-fry for 2 minutes. Add the spinach and sesame oil and stir-fry for 1 minute.

✦ Add the oyster sauce, plum sauce, sake and stock and bring to a boil, stirring continuously. Stir in the noodles, chicken and ¾ cup of the bean sprouts and stir-fry until heated through, about 3 minutes.
✦ Transfer to a serving dish. Serve immediately, topped with the remaining bean sprouts and the snow pea sprouts.

PER SERVING

487 calories / 2039 kilojoules; 39 g protein; 10.3 g fat, 22% of calories (2.3 g saturated, 4.9% of calories; 4.8 g monounsaturated, 10.2%; 3.2 g polyunsaturated, 6.9%); 53 g carbohydrate; 5.1 g dietary fiber; 556 mg sodium; 2.7 mg iron; 74 mg cholesterol.

Noodles with Roast Pork and Chinese Cabbage

CHAO SHAO CHAO MIEN

SERVES 4

4 dried Chinese mushrooms,
    about 1½ in (3 cm) wide
8 oz (250 g) fresh egg noodles
1 tablespoon peanut or corn oil
1 onion, cut into 12 wedges
1 red bell pepper (capsicum),
    thinly sliced
2 cups shredded Chinese cabbage
1 cup snow peas (mange-tout),
    trimmed
1 tablespoon reduced-sodium
    soy sauce
1 tablespoon sake (rice wine) or
    rice vinegar
½ cup (4 fl oz / 125 ml) reduced-
    sodium chicken stock,
    skimmed of fat
8 oz (250 g) Chinese roast
    pork, cut into long thin strips

Chinese noodles come in a range of shapes from flat ribbons to thin strings but they are always long, because they are a symbol of longevity. If fresh noodles are unavailable, substitute with dried noodles.

PREPARATION   *35 minutes*

✦ Place the mushrooms in a small bowl, cover with boiling water and leave to soak for 30 minutes. Drain. Trim off the stems and discard. Cut the caps into thin slices.
✦ Bring a large saucepan of water to a boil. Add the noodles and cook, stirring occasionally, until just tender, about 5 minutes. Drain.

COOKING   *10 minutes*

✦ Heat the oil in a wok or large, non-stick skillet over medium-high heat. Add the onion and stir-fry for 1 minute. Add the bell pepper and stir-fry for 2 minutes. Add the Chinese cabbage, snow peas and mushrooms and stir-fry for 1 minute.

✦ Add the soy sauce, sake and stock and bring to a boil, stirring continuously. Reduce the heat and simmer until the cabbage is soft, about 1 minute.
✦ Stir in the pork and noodles and heat through, stirring continuously. Place in a serving dish and serve immediately.

PER SERVING

352 calories / 1473 kilojoules; 25 g protein; 4.9 g fat, 15% of calories (1.1 g saturated, 3.5% of calories; 2.2 g monounsaturated, 6.6%; 1.6 g polyunsaturated, 4.9%); 49 g carbohydrate; 3.6 g dietary fiber; 216 mg sodium; 1.9 mg iron; 42 mg cholesterol.

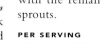

*Noodles with Roast Pork
and Chinese Cabbage*

Mussel Pilaf
MITHIA PILAFI

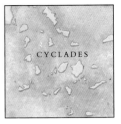

CYCLADES

SERVES 4

1 cup (7 oz/220 g) long-grain
    rice
2 lb (1 kg) mussels in the shell
1 tablespoon virgin olive oil
1 red onion, chopped
¾ cup sliced scallions (spring
    onions)
2 cups (16 fl oz/500 ml) fish
    stock or water
1 cup (8 fl oz/250 ml) dry
    white wine
¼ cup (2 fl oz/60 ml) light cream
¼ teaspoon salt
¼ teaspoon freshly ground white
    pepper
1 tablespoon freshly squeezed
    lemon juice
1 tablespoon kalamata olives,
    pitted and quartered
    lengthwise
1 tablespoon chopped oregano
1 tablespoon chopped parsley
herb sprigs, for garnish
lemon wedges, for serving

Eating on the Greek islands is an exciting experience as there is an amazing variety of fish and shellfish to choose from. Harborside *tavernas* serve dishes featuring all sorts, including sardines, red mullet, calamari, octopus, shrimp and mussels.

PREPARATION   *15 minutes*
◆ Wash the rice under cold running water and drain.
◆ Scrub and debeard the mussels.

COOKING   *40 minutes*
◆ Heat the oil in a large, heavy-bottomed saucepan over low heat. Add the onion and ½ cup of the scallions. Cook until soft, stirring occasionally, about 5 minutes.
◆ Add the mussels and stir until they begin to open. Add the stock and wine and bring to a boil. Cover and simmer for 10 minutes. Remove from the heat and, using a slotted spoon, transfer the mussels to a plate. Discard any mussels that have not opened.
◆ Add the rice to the saucepan and stir well. Return the pan to medium heat and cook, until the rice is tender, about 20 minutes. Add some water if the rice starts to dry out before it is cooked.

◆ Remove the mussel meat from the shells, then discard the shells. Lower the heat, add the mussels, remaining scallions, cream, salt and pepper to the pan, stirring continuously until heated through. Transfer to a warm serving dish.
◆ Sprinkle the lemon juice, olives, oregano and parsley over the pilaf and garnish with the herb sprigs. Serve with the lemon wedges and a salad.

PER SERVING
474 calories/1984 kilojoules; 27 g protein; 11 g fat, 24% of calories (3.9 g saturated, 8.6% of calories; 3.8 g monounsaturated, 8.2%; 3.3 g polyunsaturated, 7.2%); 53 g carbohydrate; 2.4 g dietary fiber; 509 mg sodium; 11 mg iron; 141 mg cholesterol.

Pistachio, Chicken and Rice Pilaf
FISTIKIA KOTOPOULO PILAFI

CYCLADES

SERVES 4

6½ cups (52 fl oz/1.6 l)
    reduced-sodium chicken stock,
    skimmed of fat
1 cup (7 oz/220 g) long-grain rice
2 tablespoons virgin olive oil
8 oz (250 g) boneless, skinless
    chicken thighs (thigh fillets),
    cut into ½ in (1 cm) pieces
1 onion, finely chopped
2 oz (60 g) shelled pistachio
    nuts, chopped
1 carrot, cut into julienne strips
grated zest and juice of 1 lemon
2 tablespoons thyme leaves
freshly ground black pepper, to
    taste
4 figs, quartered

The lovely green pistachio nut is one of the main agricultural products on some of the Greek islands. Serve this pilaf with a cherry tomato and arugula (rocket) salad. Adding extra pistachios will increase both the flavor and the fat level.

PREPARATION   *25 minutes*
◆ Bring 6 cups of the chicken stock to a boil. Add the rice and cook until tender, about 10 minutes.
◆ Drain and set aside.
◆ Preheat the oven to 350°F (180°C).

COOKING   *30 minutes*
◆ Heat the oil in a heavy-bottomed, flameproof casserole dish over medium heat. Add the chicken and onion and cook, stirring frequently, until both are golden, about 5 minutes.
◆ Reduce the heat to low. Add the rice, pistachio nuts, carrot, remaining stock, lemon zest and juice and thyme. Stir well.

◆ Cover and bake until heated through, about 20 minutes.
◆ Add the pepper and fold the figs gently through the pilaf.
◆ Serve immediately.

PER SERVING
417 calories/1746 kilojoules; 17 g protein; 18 g fat, 39% of calories (3.8 g saturated, 8.2% of calories; 11.1 g monounsaturated, 24.1%; 3.1 g polyunsaturated, 6.7%); 47 g carbohydrate; 5.7 g dietary fiber; 526 mg sodium; 1.3 mg iron; 65 mg cholesterol.

Mussel Pilaf

Prawn Pilaf

KONJU PILAO

SERVES 6

2½ cups (17½ oz / 550 g)
    basmati or other long-grain
    rice
1½ lb (750 g) raw shrimp
    (prawns)
6 garlic cloves, halved
2 in (5 cm) ginger
5 green chilies, halved and
    seeded
1 teaspoon ground cumin
5⅓ cups (43 fl oz / 1.34 l) water
2 tablespoons vegetable oil
¼ cup (1½ oz / 45 g) raw cashew
    nuts
1 onion, thinly sliced
2 vine-ripened tomatoes,
    chopped
½ cup (4 oz / 125 g) low-fat
    plain yogurt
½ cup (1½ oz / 45 g) grated fresh
    coconut or ¼ cup (¾ oz / 20 g)
    desiccated coconut
½ cup (4 fl oz / 125 ml) coconut
    milk
¼ teaspoon salt
1 cinnamon stick
8 cloves
5 cardamom pods
lime pickles, for serving
lime wedges, for serving

This dish was originally made by the Muslim fishermen of Kerala, a lush area on the southwest coast of India. Spices grow in abundance here and give Keralan dishes their special character and aroma.

PREPARATION   *35 minutes*

✦ Wash the rice under cold running water until the water runs clear. Drain, then place it in a bowl, cover with water and soak for 30 minutes.
✦ Shell and devein the shrimp. Refrigerate them until required.
✦ Place the garlic, ginger, chilies and cumin in a food processor or blender. Add ⅓ cup of the water and mix to form a paste.

COOKING   *50 minutes*

✦ Heat the oil in a wok or large, heavy-bottomed skillet over medium heat. Add the cashews and cook until golden, being careful not to let them burn, about 1 minute. Using a slotted spoon, transfer the cashews to a plate lined with paper towels.
✦ Add the onion to the wok and cook until soft and golden, about 5 minutes. Transfer to the plate with the cashews to drain.
✦ Add the spicy paste to the wok and cook, stirring continuously, for 2 minutes. Add the tomatoes and cook until soft, stirring continuously, about 2 minutes.
✦ Add the yogurt, reduce the heat to low and cook, stirring continuously, until the yogurt separates.

✦ Add the coconut and coconut milk and simmer for 1 minute.
✦ Add the shrimp and salt, stir well and remove from the heat. Place the shrimp mixture in a casserole dish.
✦ Preheat the oven to 325°F (165°C).
✦ Meanwhile, bring the 5 cups of water to a boil in a large saucepan. Add the rice, cinnamon, cloves and cardamom and boil rapidly, uncovered, for 8 minutes. Drain well.
✦ Place the rice evenly on top of the shrimp mixture in the casserole dish. Arrange the onions and cashews on top of the rice. Make a well in the center of the pilaf to the bottom of the dish to allow the steam to rise. Cover and bake until the rice and shrimp are cooked, about 20 minutes.
✦ Serve with the lime pickles and lime wedges.

PER SERVING
*584 calories / 2444 kilojoules; 32 g protein; 15 g fat,
24% of calories (6.7 g saturated, 10.7% of calories;
3.7 g monounsaturated, 6%; 4.6 g polyunsaturated, 7.3%);
79 g carbohydrate; 4.9 g dietary fiber; 492 mg sodium;
3.3 mg iron; 237 mg cholesterol.*

*Dwellings
lining the banks
of picturesque
Lake Pichola in
Udaipur.*

Prawn Pilaf

Rice Pancakes with Curried Winter Squash and Potato

DOSAI

DOSAI

*2 cups (14 oz/440 g) basmati
  or other long-grain rice*
⅔ cup (4⅔ oz/145 g) urad dal
¼ cup (2 fl oz/60 ml) cold water
1 teaspoon salt
1 teaspoon sugar
2 tablespoons low-fat plain yogurt
1 tablespoon vegetable oil
1 teaspoon melted ghee

**CURRIED WINTER SQUASH
AND POTATO**

1 tablespoon vegetable oil or ghee
½ teaspoon brown mustard seeds
½ teaspoon yellow mustard seeds
1 onion, finely chopped
¼ teaspoon ground turmeric
¼ teaspoon ground cumin
¼ teaspoon chili powder
*2 cups cooked cubed winter
  squash (pumpkin)*
1 cup cooked cubed potato
*½ cup (4 oz/125 g) low-fat
  plain yogurt*
*scallions (spring onions),
  for garnish*
Indian pickles, for serving

These pancakes from the south of India can be stuffed with curried split peas or vegetables and can be served at any meal. *Urad dal,* a dried white split pea sold in Indian grocery stores, is worth looking for to achieve authentic results.

PREPARATION   *30 minutes plus 12 hours standing time*
◆ Wash the rice under cold running water until the water runs clear. Drain, then place it in a medium-sized bowl, cover with water and soak for 4 hours.
◆ Place the urad dal in a small bowl, cover with water and let soak for 4 hours.
◆ Drain the rice and urad dal. Combine the rice with 1 tablespoon of the cold water in a food processor and process until finely ground. Transfer to a large mixing bowl. Process the urad dal and 1 tablespoon of the cold water in the processor until batter-like in consistency.
◆ Add the urad dal batter to the rice in the bowl. Stir in the salt and sugar. Cover and let stand at room temperature overnight. The batter will ferment slightly.

COOKING   *35 minutes*
◆ Heat the oil in a large, heavy-bottomed skillet over medium heat. Add the mustard seeds, cover and cook until the seeds start to burst.
◆ Add the onion and cook, stirring frequently, until soft, about 3 minutes.
◆ Stir in the turmeric, cumin and chili powder and cook, stirring continuously, for 1 minute.
◆ Add the winter squash and potato and stir until heated through. Add the yogurt and combine well. Remove from the heat, cover and keep hot.

◆ To make the dosai, stir the yogurt and the remaining 2 tablespoons of cold water into the prepared batter. Add more water if necessary to give the batter a runny consistency.
◆ Brush a small, non-stick skillet with a little of the oil and ghee and place the skillet over low-medium heat. Pour ⅓ of a cup of the batter into the skillet. Immediately place the rounded bottom of a spoon in the center of the skillet and spread the batter out to form a 6 in (15 cm) circle. Cover and leave to cook until golden on the bottom and firm, about 2½ minutes. Remove from the skillet and keep warm. Repeat with remaining batter to yield 8 dosai in total.
◆ Slide a dosai onto a warm dinner plate, top with some of the hot curried winter squash and potato and fold in half. Garnish with the scallions and serve with the Indian pickles.

PER SERVING
624 calories/2612 kilojoules; 19 g protein; 9.7 g fat, 14% of calories (1.9 g saturated, 2.8% of calories; 1.9 g monounsaturated, 2.8%; 5.9 g polyunsaturated, 8.4%); 114 g carbohydrate; 6.9 g dietary fiber; 542 mg sodium; 2.4 mg iron; 4 mg cholesterol.

*Rice Pancakes with
Curried Winter Squash
and Potato*

Mogul Chicken

MOGLAI MURGH

SERVES 6

1 cup (7 oz/220 g) basmati or
   other long-grain rice
1 chicken, about 3 lb (1.5 kg), cut
   into serving pieces
¼ teaspoon salt
freshly ground black pepper, to
   taste
1 tablespoon vegetable oil
1 tablespoon butter
8 cardamom pods
8 cloves
1 cinnamon stick
2 bay leaves
1 large onion, chopped
¼ cup (1 oz/30 g) slivered
   almonds
¼ cup (1¼ oz/40 g) golden
   raisins (sultanas)
1 cup (8 oz/250 g) low-fat
   plain yogurt
1 teaspoon ground cumin
½ teaspoon chili powder
1 cup (7 oz/220 g) basmati or
   other long-grain rice
3 cups (24 fl oz/750 ml) water
1 cup (8 oz/250 g) green beans,
   sliced diagonally
8 pappadams (lentil wafers),
   optional

This lightly spiced dish is from northern India. Its name reflects the influence of the Moguls who invaded India in the sixteenth century. The yogurt helps to tenderize the chicken as well as provide a tangy flavor and extra protein.

PREPARATION   *15 mintues plus 30 minutes soaking time*
✦ Wash the rice under cold running water until the water runs clear. Drain, then place it in a medium-sized bowl, cover with water and soak for 30 minutes.
✦ Remove as much skin and fat from the chicken pieces as possible, then sprinkle with the salt and pepper and set aside.
✦ Preheat the oven to 350°F (180°C).

COOKING   *55 minutes*
✦ Heat the oil and butter in a large skillet over medium heat. Add the cardamom, cloves, cinnamon, bay leaves and chicken pieces in a single layer and cook, turning once, until the chicken is browned, about 5 minutes.
✦ Using a slotted spoon, transfer the chicken pieces to a casserole dish.
✦ Reduce the heat to low, add the onion to the skillet and cook until soft, about 3 minutes. Add the almonds and golden raisins and cook, stirring, just until the raisins swell, about 1 minute. Using the slotted spoon, add the onion, almonds and raisins to the casserole dish with the chicken.

✦ Mix the yogurt with the cumin and chili powder. Pour over the chicken.
✦ Cover and bake until the juices run clear when the chicken is tested with a skewer, about 40 minutes. Stir after 20 minutes.
✦ Meanwhile, bring the water to a boil in a large saucepan. Add the rice and boil rapidly until tender, about 10 minutes. Drain well and keep hot.
✦ Steam the beans or cook in a microwave on High for 3 minutes. Stir the beans into the casserole dish with the cooked chicken.
✦ If using the pappadams, microwave in batches of 4 on High until puffed and crisp, about 1 minute.
✦ To serve, spoon the rice onto a warm serving platter with a shallow area in the center. Spoon the chicken mixture into the center of the platter and sprinkle the coarsely broken pappadams on top, if using.

PER SERVING (THIS DOES NOT INCLUDE PAPPADAMS)
407 calories/1703 kilojoules; 33 g protein; 13 g fat, 29% of calories (3.8 g saturated, 8.4% of calories; 5.6 g monounsaturated, 12.5%; 3.6 g polyunsaturated, 8.1%); 39 g carbohydrate; 3 g dietary fiber; 213 mg sodium; 2.2 mg iron; 112 mg cholesterol.

*The Red Fort
in Agra, the
ancient capital
of the Mogul
empire.*

Mogul Chicken

Spiced Saffron Rice with Lamb

SHAHJAHANI BIRYANI

1¼ cups (8½ oz/275 g) basmati
   or other long-grain rice
¼ teaspoon salt
½ teaspoon saffron threads
2 tablespoons boiling water
¼ cup (2 oz/60 g) ghee or
   unsalted butter
2 onions, thinly sliced lengthwise
¼ cup (1½ oz/45 g) raw cashew
   nuts
¼ cup (1 oz/30 g) slivered
   almonds
¼ cup (1 oz/30 g) pistachio
   nuts
2 tablespoons seedless raisins
2 teaspoons finely chopped
   ginger
1 teaspoon crushed garlic
1 teaspoon cumin seeds
¼ teaspoon cayenne pepper
2 lb (1 kg) lean boneless lamb,
   cut into 1 in (2.5 cm) cubes
1 cinnamon stick
8 cloves
6 peppercorns
4 cardamom pods
¼ teaspoon ground mace
¼ teaspoon ground nutmeg
1¼ cups (10 fl oz/300 ml)
   reduced-sodium chicken stock,
   skimmed of fat
⅔ cup (5 oz/160 g) low-fat
   plain yogurt

Muslim cuisine predominates in northern India. This northern Indian lamb recipe is named after the Mogul Emperor Shah Jahan, who built the Taj Mahal. For a Chicken Biryani, substitute a 3½ lb (1.8 kg) chicken, cut into pieces.

PREPARATION   *20 minutes*

◆ Wash the rice under cold running water until the water runs clear. Drain, then place it in a medium-sized bowl, cover with water and soak for 30 minutes.
◆ Bring a large saucepan of water to a boil. Add the rice and salt, stir well and boil rapidly, uncovered, for 10 minutes. Drain.
◆ Place the saffron in a small bowl, add the 2 tablespoons of boiling water and let soak until required.

COOKING   *1 hour and 10 minutes*

◆ Heat 3 tablespoons of the ghee in a large, flameproof casserole dish over medium heat. Add the onions and cook, stirring frequently, until soft and golden, about 5 minutes. Using a slotted spoon, transfer the onions to a plate lined with paper towels to drain.
◆ Add the cashews, almonds, pistachios and raisins to the casserole dish and sauté until the nuts are lightly browned, about 1 minute. Using a slotted spoon, transfer to a plate.
◆ Add the ginger, garlic, cumin, cayenne pepper and lamb to the casserole dish, increase the heat to medium-high and stir until the lamb is browned on all sides, about 5 minutes.
◆ Add the cinnamon, cloves, peppercorns, cardamom, mace, nutmeg, and ½ cup of the stock and bring to a boil, stirring to loosen any ingredients stuck to the bottom of the dish.
◆ Reduce the heat to low, add the yogurt and stir well. Cover and simmer for 15 minutes.
◆ Preheat the oven to 375°F (190°C).
◆ Remove the casserole dish from the heat and let stand for 5 minutes.

◆ Using a slotted spoon, transfer the lamb and cinnamon stick to a large bowl. Pour the remaining liquid into another medium-sized bowl. Wash out the casserole dish.
◆ Place the remaining ghee in the casserole dish and melt over low heat. Remove from the heat and swirl the ghee around to coat the base of the dish. Place half of the rice in the casserole dish and spread around so that it is level. Sprinkle 1 tablespoon of the saffron threads and liquid over the rice. Arrange half of the lamb on top. Place the cinnamon stick in the center.
◆ Stir the remaining stock into the cooking liquid from the lamb. Pour 1 cup of this mixture slowly down the sides of the rice in the casserole dish. Add the remaining rice and spread around so that it is level. Place the rest of the lamb on top and sprinkle with the remaining saffron mixture. Pour the remaining cooking liquid down the sides of the mixture in the casserole dish.
◆ Cover and bake until the lamb and rice are tender and most of the liquid has been absorbed, about 25 minutes.
◆ Reheat the onions, together with the nut and raisin mixture.
◆ Serve the biryani on a warm serving platter and top with the onions, nuts and raisins.

PER SERVING
430 calories/1799 kilojoules; 34 g protein; 18 g fat,
37% of calories (7.1 g saturated, 14.4% of calories;
8.5 g monounsaturated, 17.8%; 2.4 g polyunsaturated, 4.8%);
33 g carbohydrate; 2.4 g dietary fiber; 221 mg sodium;
3.3 mg iron; 100 mg cholesterol.

Stir-Fried Noodles

MI GORENG

Because Indonesia is a vast collection of islands, seafood features frequently in the country's cuisine. This dish incorporates both shrimp and beef. But other versions contain only seafood, and there are vegetarian variations as well.

SERVES 4

*4 oz (125 g) sirloin (rump)
    steak*
*1 chicken breast fillet, about
    4 oz (125 g)*
12 oz (375 g) egg noodles
2 large eggs, lightly beaten
3 tablespoons vegetable oil
3 onions, thinly sliced
3 garlic cloves, crushed
*1 small red chili, seeded and
    finely chopped*
*4 oz (125 g) small raw shrimp
    (prawns), shelled and
    deveined*
2 tablespoons soy sauce
*½ cup (4 fl oz/125 ml) chicken
    stock*
½ cup snow peas (mange-tout)
½ cup (1 oz/30 g) bean sprouts
salt, to taste
*freshly ground black pepper, to
    taste*

PREPARATION   *10 minutes*
✦ Cut the steak and the chicken breast into thin strips.

COOKING   *30 minutes*
✦ Bring a large saucepan of water to a boil. Add the noodles and cook until tender, about 5 minutes. Rinse with cold water, drain well, and set aside.
✦ Heat a small, non-stick skillet over medium heat. Add the eggs, swirl around the skillet and cook for about 30 seconds, then lift the edges of the setting omelet and tilt to allow the uncooked eggs to flow underneath. Continue cooking until the omelet is firm, about 3 minutes, then carefully slide the omelet onto a plate and allow to cool. Then cut into thin strips and set aside.
✦ Heat the oil in a large wok or skillet over medium-high heat. Add the onions, garlic and chili and stir-fry until the onions are translucent, about 3 minutes. Add the steak and chicken and stir-fry for 3 minutes.

✦ Add the shrimp, soy sauce and chicken stock and stir-fry until the steak and chicken are cooked through and the shrimp are opaque, about 5 minutes. Stir in the snow peas and bean sprouts and continue cooking until they are hot; do not overcook the snow peas.
✦ Mix in the noodles and heat through. Season with the salt and pepper. Top with the omelet strips and serve.

PER SERVING
403 calories/1687 kilojoules; 25 g protein; 12 g fat, 28% of calories (2.2 g saturated, 5% of calories; 2.9 g monounsaturated, 7%; 6.9 g polyunsaturated, 16%); 47 g carbohydrate; 3.2 g dietary fiber; 469 mg sodium; 2.4 mg iron; 135 mg cholesterol.

*A primitive
Indonesian
artwork—a carved
rock lodged in
a tree trunk.*

Savory Rice with Golden Chicken
NASI AYAM

Rice is cooked in a flavorsome chicken stock and topped with chicken, fried onions and herbs in this popular Indonesian family dish. Use free-range chicken for a more authentic flavor.

SERVES 4

2 cups (14 oz / 440 g) jasmine
  or other long-grain rice
8 small, well-shaped red chilies,
  for chili flowers
2 in (5 cm) stalk lemongrass
1 in (2 cm) galangal or ginger
½ cucumber
4 chicken breasts, about 8 oz
  (250 g) each
4 shallots (French shallots),
  chopped
3 garlic cloves, crushed
1 cinnamon stick
2 cloves
2 teaspoons ground coriander
1 teaspoon ground cumin
¼ teaspoon ground nutmeg
½ teaspoon salt
2 tablespoons peanut oil
½ cup (4 oz / 125 g) thinly sliced
  shallots (French shallots)
1 tablespoon red wine vinegar
2 tablespoons snipped chives
cilantro (coriander) sprigs,
  for garnish

PREPARATION   *20 minutes plus soaking time*

◆ Place the rice in a bowl, cover with cold water and soak for 30 minutes.
◆ Use a very sharp knife to make 2 or 3 cuts from the pointed end of each chili almost to the base of the stem end. Place each "flower" in a bowl of iced water until the "petals" curl, at least 30 minutes.
◆ Slice the lemongrass, galangal and cucumber thinly.

COOKING   *1 hour*

◆ Place the chicken, lemongrass, galangal, chopped shallots, garlic, cinnamon, cloves, ground coriander, cumin, nutmeg, and salt in a large saucepan. Add enough water to cover the chicken, at least 3 cups.
◆ Bring to a boil, then cover the saucepan, reduce the heat to low-medium, and simmer until the chicken is cooked through, about 30 minutes.
◆ Meanwhile, drain the rice. Heat 1 tablespoon of the oil in a large, heavy-bottomed saucepan over medium heat. Add the rice and cook, stirring continuously, for 5 minutes.
◆ Using a slotted spoon, remove the chicken from the stock.
◆ Add 2 cups of the stock, with flavorings, to the saucepan with the rice and bring to a boil. Reduce the heat and simmer, uncovered, until all of the stock has been absorbed, about 15 minutes. Cover and allow the rice to steam over very low heat for an additional 10 minutes.

◆ Meanwhile, preheat the broiler (grill). Line the broiler pan with aluminum foil. Place the chicken in the broiler pan and broil until hot and the skin is golden.
◆ Heat the remaining tablespoon of oil in a non-stick skillet over medium heat. Add the thinly sliced shallots, cover and cook for 4 minutes, shaking the skillet frequently while it is still in contact with the heat. Remove from the heat and stir in the vinegar.
◆ Meanwhile, slice the chicken. To serve, divide the rice among 4 plates and arrange the chicken and cucumber slices around the edge of the rice. Sprinkle the cooked shallots and chives over the rice, then garnish with the cilantro sprigs and chili "flowers."

PER SERVING
600 calories / 2511 kilojoules; 36 g protein; 11 g fat, 16% of calories (2.6 g saturated, 3.8% of calories; 5.1 g monounsaturated, 7.4%; 3.3 g polyunsaturated, 4.8%); 89 g carbohydrate; 3.3 g dietary fiber; 346 mg sodium; 1.9 mg iron; 63 mg cholesterol.

Savory Rice with Golden Chicken

Indonesian Fried Rice

NASI GORENG

SERVES 4

2 cups (14 oz / 440 g) jasmine
   or other long-grain rice
2 cups (16 fl oz / 500 ml) water
12 shrimp (prawn) crackers
1 tablespoon plus 2 teaspoons
   vegetable oil
2 large eggs, beaten
4 shallots (French shallots) or
   1 small onion, thinly sliced
2 red chilies, seeded and sliced,
   or ½ teaspoon chili powder
1 teaspoon paprika
2 slices (rashers) bacon, chopped
2 oz (60 g) Chinese roast pork,
   thinly sliced
1 carrot, cut into juliennne strips
1 cup (4 oz / 125 g) thinly sliced
   button mushrooms
1 cup (4 oz / 125 g) shredded
   Chinese cabbage
1 teaspoon reduced-sodium
   soy sauce
1 teaspoon tomato purée or sauce
2 oz (60 g) cooked baby (school)
   shrimp, peeled and deveined
sliced cucumber, for garnish
sliced tomatoes, for garnish
cilantro (coriander) sprigs, for
   garnish

In Indonesia, a basically plain but spicy *Nasi Goreng,* or fried rice, is served with meat or chicken satays and fish dishes or as part of a *rijsttafel,* an Indonesian-style buffet meal that became popular during Dutch colonial days.

PREPARATION   *30 minutes plus 2 hours cooling time*

◆ Wash the rice under cold running water. Place the rice in a large, heavy-bottomed saucepan. Add the water and bring to a boil, stirring occasionally. Boil, uncovered, until all the water has been absorbed, about 25 minutes.
◆ Reduce the heat to as low as possible, cover the saucepan and leave undisturbed for 10 minutes. Remove from the heat and let the rice cool for at least 2 hours to assure good results.
◆ Microwave the shrimp crackers in batches of 4 on High until puffed, about 30 seconds.
◆ Heat 2 teaspoons of the oil in a small skillet over medium heat. Pour in the beaten eggs, swirl around the skillet and cook for 30 seconds, then lift the edges of the setting omelet and tilt to allow the uncooked eggs to flow underneath. Continue cooking until the omlet is firm, about 3 minutes, then carefully slide the omelet onto a plate. Let cool, then roll up the omelet and slice thinly.

COOKING   *15 minutes*

◆ Place the shallots, chilies, paprika and bacon in a wok over medium heat and cook for 2 minutes.
◆ Add the remaining oil, the pork, carrot, mushrooms and cabbage and cook for 2 minutes.
◆ Add the soy sauce and tomato purée and cook for 1 minute.
◆ Add the rice to the wok and stir continuously until it is heated through, about 5 to 8 minutes.
◆ Add the shrimp and stir through the rice mixture. Transfer to a serving dish, top with the omelet strips and crumble 4 of the shimp crackers on top.
◆ Serve hot, garnished with the sliced cucumber, tomatoes, cilantro sprigs and the remaining shrimp crackers.

PER SERVING

505 calories / 2115 kilojoules; 21 g protein; 6.4 g fat, 12% of calories (1.4 g saturated, 2.6% of calories; 1.8 g monounsaturated, 3.4%; 3.2 g polyunsaturated, 6%); 90 g carbohydrate; 4.7 g dietary fiber; 829 mg sodium; 1.7 mg iron; 39 mg cholesterol.

Terraced rice paddies on the scenic island of Bali.

Indonesian Fried Rice

Orecchiette with Fresh Beans

ORECCHIETTE E FAGIOLI FRESCHI

SERVES 4

1 lb (500 g) fresh shelled fava
(broad) beans
1 tablespoon virgin olive oil
1 garlic clove, crushed
2 lb (1 kg) plum (Roma)
tomatoes, peeled and
quartered
2 cups (11 oz/330 g) orecchiette
2 tablespoons tomato paste
2 teaspoons chopped oregano
2 teaspoons shredded basil
2 tablespoons chopped parsley
freshly ground black pepper,
to taste
freshly shaved Parmesan cheese,
for garnish
basil leaves, for garnish

The fresh broad bean of summertime features in this delicious Neapolitan recipe.
It is matched with a similarly shaped pasta called orecchiette, "little ears," in a
tasty tomato sauce.

PREPARATION   *25 minutes*

✦ Bring a large saucepan of water to a boil. Add the
fava beans and cook for 3 minutes. Drain and set aside
until cool enough to handle. Peel off the outer skin.

COOKING   *30 minutes*

✦ Heat the oil over very low heat in a large, heavy-
bottomed saucepan. Add the garlic and stir until
golden, about 1 minute.
✦ Add the tomatoes, increase the heat to medium-high
and bring to a boil. Reduce the heat and simmer,
covered, until soft, about 10 minutes.
✦ Add the beans and simmer, covered, for an additional
10 minutes.
✦ Meanwhile, bring a large saucepan of water to a boil.

Add the orecchiette and cook until just tender, about
15 minutes.
✦ While the pasta is cooking, stir the tomato paste and
herbs through the tomato mixture. Add the pepper.
✦ Drain the orecchiette well and add to the hot tomato
sauce mixture, folding in gently.
✦ Serve in 4 pasta bowls, garnished with the Parmesan
cheese and basil leaves.

PER SERVING

*445 calories/1863 kilojoules; 23 g protein; 7 g fat, 15% of calories
(2.2 g saturated, 4.7% of calories; 3.3 g monounsaturated, 7.1%;
1.5 g polyunsaturated, 3.2%); 70 g carbohydrate; 16 g dietary
fiber; 140 mg sodium; 5.1 mg iron; 5 mg cholesterol.*

Fettuccine with Butter and Cheese

FETTUCCINE AL BURRO

SERVES 4

1 truffle, optional
10 oz (300 g) fresh fettuccine
3 tablespoons (1½ oz/45 g)
butter
¼ cup (2 fl oz/60 ml) skim or
soy milk
1 teaspoon saffron threads
¼ cup (2 fl oz/60 ml) light cream
1 cup (4 oz/125 g) freshly
grated Parmesan cheese
basil leaves, for garnish

Fettuccine are narrow egg noodles very similar to tagliatelle. The *al burro* sauce
is a rich butter sauce from northern Italy, made even richer with the addition of
cream. Even this lighter version of the traditional recipe is quite high in fat.

PREPARATION   *5 minutes*

✦ Finely chop the truffle, if using.

COOKING   *12 minutes*

✦ Bring a large saucepan of water to a boil. Add the
fettuccine and cook until just tender, about 5 minutes.
✦ While the fettucine is cooking, melt the butter in a
large saucepan over low heat, then add the milk.
✦ Sprinkle the saffron on top, remove from the heat
and let stand for 5 minutes.
✦ Stir in the truffle, if using, the cream and half of the
Parmesan cheese.

✦ Drain the fettuccine well and add to the warm butter mixture. Toss well.
✦ Divide the fettuccine among 4 pasta bowls and top
with the remaining Parmesan cheese. Garnish with the
basil leaves and serve immediately.

PER SERVING

*447 calories/1870 kilojoules; 20 g protein; 27 g fat, 54% of
calories (16.7 g saturated, 33% of calories; 8.5 g monounsaturated,
17%; 1.8 g polyunsaturated, 4%); 30 g carbohydrate; 1.5 g dietary
fiber; 677 mg sodium; 1.1 mg iron; 159 mg cholesterol.*

Orecchiette with Fresh Beans

Lasagne with Meat and Spinach

LASAGNE

SERVES 4

12 oz (375 g) lasagne

8 oz (250 g) frozen spinach,
    thawed and drained

1 cup (8 oz/250 g) ricotta or
    low-fat cottage cheese

¼ cup (2 oz/60 g) low-fat plain
    yogurt

¼ teaspoon ground nutmeg

1 quantity Bolognese sauce
    (see page 102)

CHEESE SAUCE

2 tablespoons butter

2 tablespoons all-purpose
    (plain) flour

2 cups (16 fl oz/500 ml)
    skim milk

¼ cup (1 oz/30 g) freshly grated
    Parmesan cheese

¼ cup (1 oz/30 g) freshly grated,
    reduced-fat mozzarella cheese

freshly ground black pepper

Lasagne is made by layering sheets of cooked pasta with various savory mixtures, then baking the casserole to blend the textures and tastes. It's an ideal dish to assemble in advance and freeze (unbaked) until the day you want to serve it.

PREPARATION   *1¼ hours, including making the sauce*

◆ Bring a very large saucepan of water to a boil. Add the pasta and cook until just tender, about 10 minutes. Remove with a slotted spoon and lay on a clean cloth. Do not let the pasta sheets touch each other.

◆ Preheat the oven to 350°F (180°C).

◆ Spray an 11 × 7 in (28 × 17 cm) lasagne dish with olive oil cooking spray.

COOKING   *50 minutes*

◆ Place the spinach, ricotta, yogurt and nutmeg in a medium-sized mixing bowl and fold with a plastic spatula until well mixed.

◆ To make the sauce, melt the butter in a small, heavy-bottomed saucepan over medium heat. Add the flour and stir continuously for 2 minutes. Add the milk, increase the heat to medium-high and bring to a boil,

stirring continuously. Add half of both of the cheeses, reduce the heat to low and stir continuously until the cheeses are melted. Season to taste with the pepper.

◆ To assemble the lasagne, spread half of the Bolognese sauce over the base of the dish. Cover with a layer of the lasagne sheets. Cover with half of the spinach mixture. Cover with another layer of lasagne sheets.

◆ Repeat these 4 layers one more time, cover with the cheese sauce, and sprinkle with the remaining cheese.

◆ Bake until bubbling hot, about 30 minutes. Serve immediately with a green salad.

PER SERVING

727 calories/3043 kilojoules; 52 g protein; 18 g fat, 23% of calories (9.9 g saturated, 12.7% of calories; 6 g monounsaturated, 7.5%; 2.1 g polyunsaturated, 2.8%); 84 g carbohydrate; 9.5 g dietary fiber; 770 mg sodium; 4.3 mg iron; 81 mg cholesterol.

Pasta with Broccoli

PENNE CON BROCCOLI

SERVES 4

2 canned anchovy fillets

2 tablespoons milk

½ cup (2 oz/60 g) golden
    raisins (sultanas)

5 cups (1 lb/500 g) broccoli florets

12 oz (375 g) penne

4 teaspoons virgin olive oil

1 small onion, sliced

1 garlic clove, finely chopped

1½ cups canned plum (Roma)
    tomatoes, chopped

½ teaspoon salt

¼ teaspoon freshly ground
    black pepper

2 tablespoons lightly toasted pine
    nuts

1 tablespoon chopped basil

½ cup (1 oz/30 g) freshly grated
    pecorino cheese

Fishing is one of the main livelihoods of the Sicilian people and fish often features in the island's dishes. Here it is combined with tomatoes and olive oil to make a traditional pasta dish.

PREPARATION   *15 minutes plus 1 hour soaking time*

◆ Soak the anchovies in the milk for 1 hour to reduce the saltiness. Drain, pat dry and chop coarsely.

◆ Place the golden raisins in a small bowl, cover with hot water and let stand for 15 minutes. Drain.

COOKING   *40 minutes*

◆ Bring a large saucepan of water to a boil. Add the broccoli and simmer until just tender, about 15 minutes. Drain well and set aside.

◆ While the broccoli is cooking, bring another large saucepan of water to a boil. Add the penne and cook until just tender, about 15 minutes.

◆ Heat 3 teaspoons of the oil in a large saucepan over medium-high heat. Add the onion and garlic and cook until softened, about 3 minutes. Add the tomatoes,

reduce the heat, cover and simmer for 10 minutes.

◆ While the sauce simmers, heat the remaining oil in a small saucepan over low heat. Add the anchovies and crush to form a smooth paste. Stir the anchovies into the tomato sauce. Add the salt and pepper, then stir in the golden raisins and pine nuts. Add the broccoli and stir gently. Remove from the heat and keep warm.

◆ Drain the penne. Place in a serving dish, top with the broccoli mixture, basil and cheese. Serve at once.

PER SERVING

537 calories/2248 kilojoules; 22 g protein; 13 g fat, 23% of calories (3.2 g saturated, 6% of calories; 5.9 g monounsaturated, 10%; 3.9 g polyunsaturated, 7%); 82 g carbohydrate; 12 g dietary fiber; 528 mg sodium; 3.9 mg iron; 9 mg cholesterol.

Lasagne with Meat and Spinach

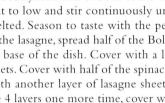

"Straw and Hay" Pasta

PAGLIA E FIENO

This pasta dish from Emilia takes its name from the combination of yellow- and green-colored fettuccine. This recipe calls for two tasty sauces to serve with the pasta, but you can save time by making only one—just double the quantities.

SERVES 4

**MUSHROOM AND
SPICY SAUSAGE SAUCE**

4 oz (125 g) Italian spicy
  sausage
2 teaspoons butter
1 garlic clove, crushed
2½ cups (8 oz/250 g) sliced
  mushroom caps
¼ cup (2 fl oz/60 ml) dry
  white wine
2 tablespoons chopped flat-leaf
  parsley
¼ cup (2 fl oz/60 ml) reduced-
  sodium chicken stock

PEA AND HAM SAUCE

1 cup (5 oz/150 g) peas
2 oz (60 g) prosciutto
2 teaspoons virgin olive oil
1 small onion, finely chopped
¼ cup (2 fl oz/60 ml) reduced-
  sodium chicken stock
¼ cup (2 fl oz/60 ml) light cream

6 oz (180 g) fettuccine
6 oz (180 g) green fettuccine
¼ cup (1 oz/30 g) freshly grated
  Parmesan cheese

PREPARATION   *30 minutes*

✦ Slit the sausage skin and remove the sausage filling. Discard the skin.
✦ Steam the peas until tender, about 15 minutes.
✦ Cut the prosciutto into thin strips.

COOKING   *20 minutes*

✦ Bring two large saucepans of water to a boil. Add one type of fettuccine to each and cook until just tender, about 10 minutes. Keep separate when draining. While the pasta is cooking, prepare the sauces.
✦ *Mushroom and Spicy Sausage Sauce*: Melt the butter in a medium-sized, non-stick skillet over medium heat. Add the garlic and mushrooms, cover and cook, shaking the pan occasionally while still in contact with the heat. Cook until the mushrooms are tender, about 5 minutes. Add the wine and parsley, stir to combine and remove from the heat. In a second small skillet over medium heat, fry the sausage meat in its own fat, stirring until it is crumbled and browned. Drain off any fat. Add the stock, bring to a boil, then remove from the heat. Combine the sausage mixture with the mushroom mixture just before serving.

✦ *Pea and Ham Sauce*: Heat the oil in a medium-sized, heavy-bottomed skillet over low heat. Add the onion and cook until soft but not brown, about 3 minutes. Add the stock, cream and peas to the skillet. Bring to a boil. Stir in the prosciutto just before serving.
✦ Add the plain-colored pasta to the mushroom and spicy sausage sauce, add the green pasta to the pea and ham sauce and toss both gently in their skillets. Heat through if necessary.
✦ Serve the pastas side by side on a large, warm platter, or serve side by side in individual pasta bowls, accompanied by the Parmesan cheese for each diner to sprinkle on top.

PER SERVING
*526 calories/2202 kilojoules; 24 g protein; 20 g fat,
34% of calories (9.8 g saturated, 16.7% of calories;
8.2 g monounsaturated, 13.9%; 2 g polyunsaturated, 3.4%);
60 g carbohydrate; 7.5 g dietary fiber; 657 mg sodium;
3 mg iron; 60 mg cholesterol.*

*New and old
craft ply the
canals of Venice.*

"Straw and Hay" Pasta

Spaghetti with Bolognese Sauce
SPAGHETTI ALLA BOLOGNESE

BOLOGNESE SAUCE

1¾ cups (13 oz/410 g) canned
    plum (Roma) tomatoes
4 teaspoons virgin olive oil
1 carrot, finely chopped
1 stalk celery, finely chopped
1 onion, finely chopped
8 oz (250 g) finely ground
    (minced) lean beef
8 oz (250 g) finely ground
    (minced) lean pork
1 cup (8 fl oz/250 ml) reduced-
    sodium beef stock
½ cup (4 fl oz/125 ml) dry
    white or red wine
2 tablespoons tomato paste
1 bay leaf
¼ teaspoon salt
freshly ground black pepper

12 oz (375 g) spaghetti
2 oz/60 g Parmesan cheese

This famous dish comes from Bologna, a city famous for its rich cooking style, and Bolognese sauce is traditionally made with bacon, pork, beef, chicken livers and cream. This recipe has been tempered to cut down on fat.

PREPARATION   *10 minutes*
✦ Cut up the tomatoes with kitchen scissors. Reserve all of the juice.
✦ Grate the Parmesan cheese.

COOKING   *45 minutes*
✦ Heat the oil in a large, heavy-bottomed skillet over medium heat. Add the carrot, celery and onion and cook, stirring frequently, for 5 minutes.
✦ Add the ground beef and pork and stir continuously with a wooden spoon until browned.
✦ Add the stock, tomatoes and their juice and the wine and bring to a boil, stirring to loosen any ingredients stuck to the bottom of the pan. Add the tomato paste, bay leaf and salt, cover and simmer, stirring occasionally, for 30 minutes.

✦ Meanwhile, bring a large saucepan of water to a boil. Add the spaghetti and cook until just tender, about 10 to 12 minutes. Drain well and keep hot.
✦ Remove the bay leaf from the sauce and season to taste with the pepper. If the sauce is too thin, simmer, uncovered, until it has reduced a little.
✦ Divide the spaghetti among 4 warm pasta bowls. Spoon the sauce over the spaghetti and sprinkle with the Parmesan cheese.

PER SERVING

573 calories/2398 kilojoules; 42 g protein; 12 g fat, 19% of calories (4.3 g saturated, 6.8% of calories; 6 g monounsaturated, 9.5%; 1.7 g polyunsaturated, 2.7%); 68 g carbohydrate; 6.8 g dietary fiber; 517 mg sodium; 3.9 mg iron; 76 mg cholesterol.

Pasta with Eggplant and Tomato Sauce
RIGATONI ALLA NORMA

3 eggplants (aubergines), thinly
    sliced crosswise
1½ tablespoons plus ¼ teaspoon
    salt
12 oz (375 g) vine-ripened
    tomatoes
2¾ cups (12 oz/375 g) rigatoni
3 tablespoons virgin olive oil
⅓ cup chopped basil
2 garlic cloves, finely chopped
¼ teaspoon freshly ground
    black pepper
½ cup (2 oz/60 g) freshly grated
    Parmesan cheese
basil sprigs, for garnish

Sicilians often serve pasta *con le melanzane,* with a sauce made of tomatoes and eggplants. The town of Catania renamed this sauce *alla Norma,* to commemorate the opera *Norma,* composed by the locally born Vincenzo Bellini.

PREPARATION   *10 minutes plus 1 hour draining time*
✦ Sprinkle the eggplant slices with 1½ tablespoons of the salt, place in a colander and leave to drain for 1 hour. Then rinse well and pat dry with paper towels.
✦ Place the tomatoes in a bowl and cover with boiling water. Let stand until the skins begin to split, about 10 minutes. Remove the tomatoes from the bowl, peel, cut in half crosswise and scoop out the seeds. Purée the flesh in a blender or food processor.

COOKING   *20 minutes*
✦ Bring a large saucepan of water to a boil. Add the rigatoni and cook until just tender, about 15 minutes.
✦ Meanwhile, heat 1 tablespoon of the oil in a large skillet over medium-high heat. Add one-third of the eggplant slices and cook until they are brown on both sides, about 5 minutes. Remove, drain well on paper

towels and keep warm. Cook the remaining eggplant slices in the same manner.
✦ Place the tomato purée, basil, garlic, the remaining salt and pepper in a medium-sized saucepan and cook, stirring occasionally, until the sauce is quite thick, about 5 minutes.
✦ Drain the rigatoni well and place on a serving dish. Arrange the eggplant slices on top, cover with the tomato sauce, and sprinkle with the Parmesan cheese. Garnish with the basil sprigs and serve immediately.

PER SERVING

354 calories/1480 kilojoules; 13 g protein; 13 g fat, 30% of calories (4.2 g saturated, 9.6% of calories; 6.9 g monounsaturated, 15.9%; 1.9 g polyunsaturated, 4.5%); 48 g carbohydrate; 6.8 g dietary fiber; 619 mg sodium; 1.3 mg iron; 10 mg cholesterol.

Pasta with Eggplant and Tomato Sauce

Sicilian Vermicelli with Eggplant, Anchovies and Olives

VERMICELLI ALLA SICILIANA

SERVES 4

1 eggplant (aubergine) about
    1 lb (500 g), diced
1 red or yellow bell pepper
    (capsicum)
4 canned anchovy fillets
¼ cup (2 fl oz/60 ml) milk
1 tablespoon virgin olive oil
2 garlic cloves, crushed
6 large vine-ripened tomatoes,
    cut into 12 wedges
13 oz (400 g) vermicelli
1 tablespoon capers
¼ cup (2½ oz/75 g) black olives
2 tablespoons shredded basil
basil sprigs, for garnish

Sicilian cooking is close to that of Greece, as is apparent in this dish featuring eggplant, anchovies and olives. Interestingly the Sicilians were making pasta, which they called "maccaruni," long before the inhabitants of the rest of Italy.

PREPARATION   *20 minutes*

✦ Preheat the broiler (grill).
✦ Place the diced eggplant in a colander, sprinkle with salt and let stand for 10 minutes, then drain off the bitter juices. This process is not necessary if the eggplant is young or freshly picked from the garden.
✦ Meanwhile, cut the bell pepper in half lengthwise and remove the seeds and white membrane.
✦ Broil (grill) the bell pepper halves, skin side up, until the skin is charred and blistered, about 5 minutes. Place the peppers in a clean, plastic bag, seal, cover with a cloth and leave for 5 minutes. Rub the skin off the pepper halves with your fingers.
✦ Rinse the anchovies in the milk, then chop.

COOKING   *25 minutes*

✦ Heat the oil in a large, non-stick saucepan over medium heat. Add the garlic and eggplant, cover and cook for 1 minute. Stir well, reduce the heat to low, cover and cook for 5 minutes, shaking the pan frequently while still in contact with the heat source.
✦ Add the tomatoes and bring to a boil, stirring continuously. Cover and simmer until the tomatoes are soft and juicy, about 10 minutes.

✦ Meanwhile, bring a large saucepan of water to a boil. Add the vermicelli and cook until just tender, about 10 minutes.
✦ While the pasta is cooking, add the bell peppers, anchovies, capers and olives to the tomato mixture. Cover and simmer for 5 minutes. Stir in the shredded basil.
✦ Drain the vermicelli well. Return to the saucepan. Add half of the sauce and toss gently to coat well.
✦ Divide the vermicelli among 4 pasta bowls and spoon the remaining sauce on top. Garnish with the basil sprigs and serve immediately.

PER SERVING
384 calories/1605 kilojoules; 14 g protein; 7.8 g fat, 19% of calories (1.3 g saturated, 3.2% of calories; 5.4 g monounsaturated, 13.1%; 1.1 g polyunsaturated, 2.7%); 63 g carbohydrate; 9.6 g dietary fiber; 679 mg sodium; 1.8 mg iron; 3 mg cholesterol.

Sicilian Vermicelli with Eggplant,
Anchovies and Olives

Pasta Shells with Eggplant, Tomato and Cauliflower
CONCHIGLIE MELANZANE E CAVOLFIORE

It was in Sicily that Greek, Roman, Arab, French and Spanish culinary influences merged. The backbone of Sicilian cuisine is pasta combined with local ingredients. Here eggplants, tomatoes and cauliflower are matched with pasta shells.

SERVES 4

4 baby or Japanese eggplants
   (aubergines), about 11 oz/350 g
2 tablespoons plus 2 teaspoons
   virgin olive oil
13 oz (400 g) pasta shells
2 garlic cloves, crushed
1½ lb (750 g) vine-ripened
   tomatoes, coarsely chopped
2 tablespoons shredded basil
1 tablespoon chili sauce
½ teaspoon brown sugar
freshly ground black pepper,
   to taste
2 cups (8 oz/250 g) cauliflower
   florets
basil sprigs, for garnish
¼ cup (1 oz/30 g) freshly grated
   Parmesan cheese

PREPARATION   *10 minutes*
+ Cut the eggplants into ½ in (1 cm) thick slices.

COOKING   *20 minutes*
+ Heat the 2 tablespoons of oil in a large, non-stick skillet over medium heat. Add the eggplant slices, cover and cook for 1 minute. Turn the eggplant slices over, cover, reduce the heat to very low and cook for 5 minutes, shaking the skillet frequently while still in contact with the heat source. Using a slotted spoon, transfer to a plate lined with paper towels to drain.
+ Bring a large saucepan of water to a boil. Add the pasta and cook until just tender, about 10 minutes.
+ Meanwhile, heat the remaining oil in a large saucepan over low heat. Add the garlic and sauté for 30 seconds. Add the tomatoes, cover and simmer for 5 minutes. Stir in the basil, chili sauce, sugar and pepper.

+ Place the cauliflower florets in a clean, plastic bag, twist to seal and cook in a microwave oven on High for 3 minutes. Alternatively, steam until tender.
+ Add the eggplant and cauliflower to the tomato sauce, stir gently and heat until bubbling hot.
+ Drain the pasta and divide among 4 pasta bowls. Spoon the sauce on top. Garnish with the basil sprigs and serve the grated Parmesan cheese on the side.

PER SERVING
515 calories/2157 kilojoules; 19 g protein; 14 g fat, 25% of calories (3.8 g saturated, 6.7% of calories; 8.1 g monounsaturated, 14.5%; 2.1 g polyunsaturated, 3.8%); 78 g carbohydrate; 11 g dietary fiber; 154 mg sodium; 2.2 mg iron; 7 mg cholesterol.

Gnocchi Roman-Style
GNOCCHI ALLA ROMANA

Gnocchi have been a popular part of Italian cuisine since the days of ancient Rome. This version calls for instant polenta flour which does not require lengthy cooking and gives good results.

SERVES 4

4 cups (32 fl oz/1 l) water
1⅓ cups (8 oz/250 g) instant
   polenta flour
2 large eggs, lightly beaten
1 cup (4 oz/125 g) freshly
   grated Parmesan cheese
2 tablespoons (1 oz/30 g) butter

PREPARATION   *5 minutes*
+ Lightly spray a baking sheet and shallow baking dish with olive oil cooking spray.

COOKING   *45 minutes plus 1 hour cooling time*
+ Bring the water to a boil in a large, heavy-bottomed saucepan. Reduce the heat to medium.
+ Slowly sprinkle the polenta into the boiling water, stirring continuously. Reduce the heat to low and stir continuously until the polenta forms a thick mass, stiff enough to hold a wooden spoon upright, about 2 to 3 minutes. Remove from the heat.
+ Add the eggs, ¾ cup of the Parmesan cheese and half of the butter and beat well with a wooden spoon.
+ Place the mixture on the baking sheet and spread

with the back of a metal spoon to make a layer ¼ in (5 mm) thick. Refrigerate until firm, about 1 hour.
+ Preheat the oven to 400°F (200°C).
+ Using a 1 in (2 cm) pastry cutter, cut the mixture into small rounds. Place in the prepared baking dish, overlapping the rounds slightly. Sprinkle with the remaining cheese and dot with the remaining butter.
+ Bake until golden brown and crisp, about 15 minutes. Brown under a broiler (grill) to finish, if desired.
+ Serve at once, while hot and crisp.

PER SERVING
433 calories/1811 kilojoules; 20 g protein; 20 g fat, 42% of calories (12.4 g saturated, 26% of calories; 5.9 g monounsaturated, 12.6%; 1.7 g polyunsaturated, 3.4%); 43 g carbohydrate; 1.8 g dietary fiber; 537 mg sodium; 1 mg iron; 135 mg cholesterol.

Vermicelli with Mussels and Clams

VERMICELLI CON LE COZZE E LE VONGOLE

SERVES 6

2 lb (1 kg) black mussels
2 lb (1 kg) small clams
¼ cup (2 oz/60 g) salt
6 canned anchovy fillets
¼ cup (2 fl oz/60 ml) milk
2 tablespoons virgin olive oil
4 garlic cloves, crushed
1 onion, chopped
4 large vine-ripened tomatoes,
chopped
1 lb (500 g) vermicelli
freshly ground black pepper,
to taste
3 tablespoons chopped parsley

Many seafood, tomato and pasta dishes can be enjoyed along the Campania coast of southern Italy and this dish is a special treat from Naples. Traditionally it uses both mussels and clams, but it is still delicious if only one type of shellfish is available.

PREPARATION   *30 minutes plus 1 hour standing time*

✦ Scrub the mussels and remove the beards. Scrub the clams, then rinse well. Place the salt in a large bowl, add the mussels and clams and enough cold water to cover. Stir well and leave to stand in the refrigerator for 1 hour. Drain and rinse in fresh water to remove the salt.

✦ Rinse the anchovy fillets in the milk. Drain and chop.

COOKING   *30 minutes*

✦ Heat 1 tablespoon of the oil in a large saucepan over low heat. Add half the crushed garlic and cook, stirring, for 1 minute. Add the mussels and clams, increase the heat to medium, cover and cook, shaking the pan frequently, until the mussel and clam shells open, about 5 minutes. Remove from the heat.

✦ Remove the mussels and clams from their shells and discard the shells. Return the shellfish to the pan juices and set aside.

✦ Heat the remaining oil in a large, heavy-bottomed skillet over low heat. Add the anchovies, onion and remaining garlic and cook until the onion is soft, about 5 minutes. Add the tomatoes, increase the heat to medium and cook, stirring frequently, for 5 minutes. Cover, reduce the heat and simmer for 10 minutes.

✦ Meanwhile, bring a large saucepan of water to a boil. Add the vermicelli and cook until just tender, about 10 minutes.

✦ Add the shellfish and their pan juices to the skillet with the tomatoes and heat through gently (boiling will toughen the shellfish). Add the pepper.

✦ Drain the pasta and place in a large serving bowl. Pour the hot shellfish mixture over the top and combine gently. Sprinkle with the parsley and serve immediately, with warm Italian bread and a green salad.

PER SERVING
424 calories/1776 kilojoules; 25 g protein; 6 g fat, 18% of calories (1 g saturated, 3% of calories; 4 g monounsaturated, 12%; 1 g polyunsaturated, 3%); 62 g carbohydrate; 6 g dietary fiber; 316 mg sodium; 6 mg iron; 124 mg cholesterol.

The beachfront at Positano, with the hillside houses looking out onto the Bay of Salerno.

Bucatini with Tomatoes, Pork and Chili

BUCATINI ALL'AMATRICIANA

4 oz (125 g) pork or veal fillet
11 oz (350 g) bucatini
1 tablespoon virgin olive oil
1 dried red chili, crushed
2 garlic cloves, crushed
2 onions, thinly sliced
½ cup (4 fl oz/125 ml) dry
  white wine
1 lb (500 g) vine-ripened
  tomatoes, coarsely chopped
2 tablespoons chopped parsley
¼ cup (1 oz/30 g) freshly grated
  Parmesan cheese
¼ cup (1 oz/30 g) freshly grated
  pecorino cheese
flat-leaf parsley, for garnish

This Roman specialty is made with thick, hollow spaghetti called bucatini. In this recipe lean pork or veal fillet replaces the traditional salt pork in order to reduce the sodium content. Chili, onions, tomatoes and wine give the sauce great flavor.

PREPARATION   *15 minutes*
✦ Trim and dice the meat.

COOKING   *15 minutes*
✦ Bring a large saucepan of water to a boil. Add the bucatini and cook until just tender, about 10 minutes.
✦ Meanwhile, heat the oil in a large, non-stick skillet. Add the chili and garlic, cover and cook over low heat for 1 minute.
✦ Add the onions, increase the heat to medium and cook, stirring frequently, until the onions are soft and golden but not browned, about 4 minutes.
✦ Add the meat to the skillet and cook until browned on all sides, about 2 minutes.

✦ Add the wine and simmer for 2 minutes. Add the tomatoes, cover and cook until soft, about 5 minutes. Add the chopped parsley and stir through.
✦ Drain the pasta, add to the sauce together with the cheeses and toss together lightly. Garnish with the flat-leaf parsley and serve immediately.

PER SERVING
474 calories/1984 kilojoules; 24 g protein; 9.7 g fat, 19% of calories (4.1 g saturated, 8% of calories; 4.3 g monounsaturated, 8.4%; 1.3 g polyunsaturated, 2.6%); 66 g carbohydrate; 6.9 g dietary fiber; 226 mg sodium; 2 mg iron; 29 mg cholesterol.

Spaghetti with Mushrooms

SPAGHETTI CON I FUNGHI

5 cups/1 lb (500 g) fresh
  mushrooms
¼ cup dried porcini mushrooms
  (cèpes)
13 oz (400 g) thin spaghetti
1 tablespoon virgin olive oil
1 tablespoon butter
1 small onion, finely chopped
½ cup thinly sliced scallion
  (spring onion) greens
1 cup (8 fl oz/250 ml)
  vegetable stock
2 tablespoons chopped parsley
1 tablespoon brandy, optional
2 thin slices prosciutto, cut into
  julienne strips
parsley leaves, for garnish

This dish is enjoyed throughout Italy. You can use any type of fresh mushroom, but dried porcini will give it extra richness. The drying process intensifies the flavour of porcini to a remarkable degree.

PREPARATION   *15 minutes*
✦ Clean the fresh mushrooms with a dry pastry brush, then slice thinly. Do not wash them.
✦ Soak the dried porcini in boiling water for 5 minutes, then drain and set aside.

COOKING   *15 minutes*
✦ Bring a large saucepan of water to a boil. Add the spaghetti and cook until just tender, about 10 minutes.
✦ While the pasta is cooking, heat the oil and butter in a large, non-stick skillet over low heat. Add the onion and cook, stirring occasionally, until soft and transparent, about 3 minutes.
✦ Add the fresh mushrooms and scallion greens, increase the heat to medium-high and cook, stirring frequently, until the mushrooms are lightly browned, about 2 minutes.

✦ Add the stock and bring to a boil, then reduce the heat and simmer. Slice the reserved porcini, then add to the skillet with the chopped parsley and the brandy, if using. Heat through gently.
✦ Drain the spaghetti and divide among 4 pasta bowls. Spoon the mushroom sauce on top. Sprinkle the prosciutto over the top, garnish with the parsley leaves and serve immediately.

PER SERVING
466 calories/1950 kilojoules; 19 g protein; 8.5 g fat, 17% of calories (3.3 g saturated, 6.6% of calories; 3.9 g monounsaturated, 7.8%; 1.3 g polyunsaturated, 2.6%); 75 g carbohydrate; 11 g dietary fiber; 80 mg sodium; 1.9 mg iron; 8 mg cholesterol.

Bucatini with Tomatoes, Pork and Chili

Fettuccine with Fresh Tomato Sauce, Peppers and Broccoli
FETTUCCINE DI POMODORO FRESCA ABRUZZO

SERVES 4

3 thin slices smoked pancetta
1 tablespoon virgin olive oil
1 large onion, cut into 12
   wedges
2 garlic cloves, crushed
1 red bell pepper (capsicum),
   cut into thin strips
2 lb (1 kg) vine-ripened
   tomatoes, chopped
1½ cups (12 oz/375 g) broccoli
   florets
freshly ground black pepper,
   to taste
1 tablespoon shredded mint
1 lb (500 g) fettuccine
herb sprigs, for garnish
freshly grated pecorino cheese,
   for serving

The Abruzzo region of central Italy enjoys a reputation for rich, prolonged feasts. This pasta dish is one of the local specialties, adapted to appeal to the more health-conscious palates of today. Use regular pancetta if smoked is not available.

PREPARATION   *15 minutes*
✦ Cut the smoked pancetta into thin strips.

COOKING   *30 minutes*
✦ Heat the oil in a large, heavy-bottomed skillet over low heat. Add the pancetta, onion and garlic and cook, stirring occasionally, until the onion is soft and golden, about 5 minutes. Add the bell pepper and tomatoes and bring to a boil, stirring frequently. Cover and simmer for 10 minutes. Add the broccoli and pepper, then cover and simmer for 10 minutes. Stir in the mint.
✦ Meanwhile, bring a large saucepan of water to a boil.

Add the fettuccine and cook until just tender, about 10 minutes. Drain well and place in a serving bowl.
✦ Pour the sauce over the hot pasta. Garnish with the herb sprigs and serve the grated pecorino in a bowl for sprinkling on top.

PER SERVING
627 calories/2626 kilojoules; 25 g protein; 14 g fat, 23% of calories (5 g saturated, 37% of calories; 7 g monounsaturated, 12%; 2 g polyunsaturated, 3%); 95 g carbohydrate; 11 g dietary fiber; 133 mg sodium; 3 mg iron; 25 mg cholesterol.

Cannelloni Stuffed with Spinach and Ricotta
CANNELLONI VERDI

SERVES 4

8 cannelloni shells
1 onion, finely chopped
2 teaspoons virgin olive oil
8 oz (250 g) frozen spinach,
   thawed and drained
12 oz (375 g) reduced-fat
   ricotta cheese
½ cup (4 oz/125 g) low-fat
   plain yogurt
2 tablespoons pine nuts
¼ teaspoon salt
freshly ground black pepper
2 cups Neapolitan tomato sauce
   (page 36) or your favorite
   bottled sauce
1 cup (4 oz/125 g) freshly
   grated, reduced-fat
   mozzarella cheese
2 tablespoons freshly grated
   Parmesan cheese

Cannelloni are large stuffed pasta tubes that are coated with sauce and baked. The filling can be meat, chicken or cheese. Even this lighter version with its spinach and ricotta filling and the famous tomato sauce of Naples is still quite rich.

PREPARATION   *45 minutes including making the sauce*
✦ Bring a very large saucepan of water to a boil. Add the cannelloni shells and cook until just tender, about 10 minutes. Remove the shells carefully with a slotted spoon, and lay on a clean cloth, being careful not to let the shells touch each other.
✦ Preheat the oven to 350°F (180°C).
✦ Spray an 11 × 7 in (28 × 17 cm) baking dish (a lasagne dish is perfect) with olive oil cooking spray.

COOKING   *40 minutes*
✦ Heat the oil in a medium-sized, non-stick skillet over low heat. Add the onion and cook, stirring frequently.
✦ Add the spinach, stir well, then remove from the heat.
✦ Add the ricotta, yogurt, pine nuts and salt. Mix well. Season to taste with the pepper.
✦ Spread 1 cup of the tomato sauce over the base of the prepared baking dish.

✦ Using a teaspoon, spoon the ricotta mixture into the cannelloni shells. Place the filled shells in a single layer along the center of the baking dish. Cover with the remaining sauce.
✦ Sprinkle the mozzarella cheese over the shells, followed by the Parmesan.
✦ Bake until golden and bubbling hot, about 30 minutes. Serve immediately with a crisp green salad and warm Italian bread.

PER SERVING
448 calories/1874 kilojoules; 30 g protein; 26 g fat, 54% of calories (11.6 g saturated, 24.3% of calories; 9.5 g monounsaturated, 20%; 4.9 g polyunsaturated, 9.7%); 21 g carbohydrate; 6.3 g dietary fiber; 717 mg sodium; 2.7 mg iron; 69 mg cholesterol.

Fettuccine with Fresh Tomato Sauce, Peppers and Broccoli

Rigatoni with Anchovy Crumbs and Asparagus

RIGATONI AMMUDDICATA E ASPARAGI

Bread baked in a wood-fired oven and anchovies are both typical of the cooking of Calabria. This famous dish combines the two (though the bread is made into crumbs). Salted anchovies are available from Italian specialty food stores.

SERVES 4

4 salted anchovies or 8 canned anchovy fillets
¼ cup (2 fl oz/60 ml) milk
16–20 (about 1 lb/500g) asparagus spears
1 cup (4 oz/125 g) bread crumbs from day-old Italian bread
2 tablespoons virgin olive oil
1 tablespoon chili sauce
½ teaspoon brown sugar
grated zest of 1 lime
2 tablespoons freshly squeezed lime juice
2 cups (11 oz/330 g) rigatoni
½ cup (2 oz/60 g) freshly grated Parmesan or pecorino cheese
herb sprigs, for garnish

PREPARATION   20 minutes plus soaking

✦ Preheat the oven to 350°F (180°C).
✦ Place the anchovies in a small bowl, add the milk and leave to soak for 5 minutes. Drain and chop.
✦ Trim the asparagus spears and cut them into 1½ in (3 cm) lengths.

COOKING   30 minutes

✦ Spread the bread crumbs over a baking sheet. Bake until golden and crisp, about 10 to 15 minutes, stirring after 8 minutes. Cover with aluminum foil to keep warm.
✦ Meanwhile, place the asparagus pieces in a clean, plastic bag, twist to seal and cook in a microwave oven on High for 3 minutes. Alternatively, steam until tender.
✦ Heat the oil in a large saucepan over medium heat. Add the anchovies and cook, stirring continuously, until a paste is formed, about 5 minutes.

✦ Remove from the heat and stir in the chili sauce, sugar, lime zest and juice.
✦ Meanwhile, bring a large saucepan of water to a boil. Add the rigatoni and cook until just tender, about 15 minutes. Reserve 2 tablespoons of the pasta water and add to the anchovy sauce, then drain the pasta well.
✦ Add the hot pasta to the anchovy mixture and toss well. Return to a low heat to heat through if necessary. Fold in half of the bread crumbs and all of the asparagus.
✦ Place on a warm serving dish, sprinkle with the remaining bread crumbs and the Parmesan cheese and garnish with the herb sprigs. Serve immediately.

PER SERVING

541 calories/2264 kilojoules; 22 g protein; 14 g fat, 24% of calories (4.9 g saturated, 8.4% of calories; 7.2 g monounsaturated, 12.2%; 1.9 g polyunsaturated, 3.4%); 79 g carbohydrate; 7.4 g dietary fiber; 706 mg sodium; 2.8 mg iron; 21 mg cholesterol.

Looking down on the Piazza San Pietro and the River Tiber from the rooftop of Saint Peter's Basilica in Rome.

Rigatoni with Anchovy Crumbs and Asparagus

Spaghetti with Bacon, Eggs and Ricotta
SPAGHETTI ALLA CARBONARA

SERVES 4

2 slices (rashers) lean bacon
2 slices prosciutto
11 oz (350 g) spaghetti
3 teaspoons virgin olive oil
1 garlic clove, crushed
2 large eggs
1 cup (8 oz/250 g) low-fat
    ricotta cheese
¼ cup (1 oz/30 g) freshly grated
    pecorino cheese
¼ cup (1 oz/30 g) freshly grated
    Parmesan cheese
freshly ground black pepper,
    to taste

This favorite spaghetti dish comes from the mountainous region behind Rome where it was made by the *carbonari*, or charcoal burners, who worked in the forests. This is a lower-fat version of the traditional recipe.

PREPARATION   *10 minutes*
✦ Using kitchen scissors, cut the bacon into dice and cut the prosciutto into long julienne strips.

COOKING   *15 minutes*
✦ Bring a large saucepan of water to a boil. Add the spaghetti and cook until just tender, about 10 minutes.
✦ Meanwhile, heat the oil in a large, non-stick saucepan over low heat. Add the bacon and garlic and cook, stirring frequently, for 5 minutes. Do not let the garlic brown or it will give a bitter taste to the sauce.
✦ Beat the eggs with a fork in a medium-sized mixing bowl. Add the ricotta, pecorino and Parmesan cheeses. Combine well.
✦ Add the egg mixture to the saucepan, reduce the

heat to low and heat through, stirring occasionally. Add the pepper to taste.
✦ Drain the pasta well and add to the hot sauce. Toss together lightly. Divide among 4 pasta bowls and serve immediately.

PER SERVING
576 calories/2409 kilojoules; 34 g protein; 21 g fat, 33% of calories (10.6 g saturated, 16.5% of calories; 8.3 g monounsaturated, 13.2%; 2.1 g polyunsaturated, 3.3%); 62 g carbohydrate; 4.5 g dietary fiber; 1004 mg sodium; 1.6 mg iron; 162 mg cholesterol.

Farfalle with Tangy Smoked Salmon
FARFALLE E SALMONE AFFUMICATO

SERVES 4

1 teaspoon saffron threads
1 tablespoon hot water or dry
    white wine
6½ oz (200 g) thinly sliced
    smoked salmon
¾ cup (6 oz/180 g) low-fat
    plain yogurt
2 tablespoons light cream
2 tablespoons snipped chives
    or thinly sliced scallions
    (spring onions)
2 tablespoons chopped dill or
    mint
finely grated zest of 1 lemon
2 tablespoons freshly squeezed
    lemon juice
12 oz (375 g) farfalle pasta
dill or mint sprigs, for garnish

In this easy recipe, elegant pasta butterflies, or bows, are dressed with a saffron- and herb-scented yogurt sauce and topped with delicious strips of smoked salmon. This dish is ideal for a summer's lunch.

PREPARATION   *10 minutes*
✦ Soak the saffron threads in the hot water.
✦ Cut the smoked salmon into strips 1 in (2 cm) wide.

COOKING   *15 minutes*
✦ Place the yogurt, saffron and saffron liquid in a small bowl and mix well.
✦ Add the cream, herbs, lemon zest and juice and fold together with a plastic spatula.
✦ Bring a large saucepan of water to a boil. Add the farfalle and cook until just tender, about 10 minutes. Take care not to overcook as the tips of the "bows" are delicate. Drain well.

✦ Return the farfalle to the saucepan, away from the heat, add the yogurt mixture and fold together until the pasta is coated, being careful not to let the mixture cook.
✦ Divide the pasta among 4 pasta bowls. Top each portion with the strips of salmon. Garnish with the dill sprigs and serve immediately.

PER SERVING
417 calories/1745 kilojoules; 25 g protein; 5.4 g fat, 12% of calories (2.2 g saturated, 4.9% of calories; 1.7 g monounsaturated, 3.7%; 1.5 g polyunsaturated, 3.4%); 65 g carbohydrate; 4.6 g dietary fiber; 911 mg sodium; 1.2 mg iron; 31 mg cholesterol.

Farfalle with Tangy Smoked Salmon

Sushi

NORIMAKI ZUSHI

MAKES 64

3⅓ cups (1½ lb/750 g)
    short-grain rice
5½ tablespoons rice vinegar
5 tablespoons sugar
4 teaspoons salt
4 cups (32 fl oz/1 l) water
8 sheets nori (dried seaweed)
2 oz (60 g) pickled ginger,
    thinly sliced
1¼ oz (50 g) pickled daikon
    (Japanese radish), thinly
    sliced

FILLING

8 oz (250 g) sushi-grade tuna
10 large cooked shrimp
    (prawns), shelled, deveined
    and halved lengthwise
1 cucumber
1 large young carrot
1 large avocado
juice of 1 lime or ½ lemon,
    freshly squeezed

Japanese sushi bars are becoming increasingly popular, but hand-rolled sushi can be made successfully at home for a delicious party savory. Serve them with wasabi paste (Japanese horseradish), tamari and chili dipping sauces.

PREPARATION   *45 minutes plus 2 hours standing time*

✦ Wash the rice under cold running water until the water runs clear. Drain in a fine colander for at least 1 hour.

✦ Combine the rice vinegar, sugar and salt in a small saucepan and cook over very low heat, stirring continuously, until the sugar dissolves. Remove from the heat and let cool.

✦ Place the rice in a rice cooker or in a large saucepan with a tight-fitting lid, and add the water. Cover tightly and bring to a boil. Boil for 2 minutes, then reduce the heat to very low. Cook until all the water has been absorbed, about 15 minutes. Remove from the heat and take off the lid. Spread a clean towel over the top of the saucepan, replace the lid loosely and let stand for about 15 minutes.

✦ Empty the cooked rice into a shallow wooden bowl (or other non-metallic bowl). Run chopsticks through the rice to separate the grains while gradually adding the vinegar mixture. Add only enough of the mixture to moisten the rice without making it too wet. Cover the rice and allow to cool for at least 1 hour.

✦ Meanwhile, slice the tuna into long strips, about ¼ in (5 mm) wide. Cut the shrimp into long thin strips. Cut the cucumber in half lengthwise and remove the seeds. Cut the carrot and cucumber into ¼ in (5 mm) matchsticks. Peel and pit the avocado, and cut it into thin wedges, brushing them with the lime juice to prevent browning.

✦ Toast the sheets of nori by passing each one quickly through a gas flame or by holding over an electric hotplate for 2 seconds.

ASSEMBLY   *30 minutes*

✦ Place a sheet of nori on a bamboo sushi mat. Wet your hands in a bowl of salted water to prevent the rice from sticking. Spread one-eighth of the rice over the nori, leaving a 2 in (5 cm) border along the top edge.

✦ Place one-eighth of the tuna strips lengthwise in a row on top of the rice along the edge nearest to you. Follow this with rows of one-eighth of each of the shrimp, cucumber, carrot and avocado. Top with slices of the pickled ginger and daikon.

✦ Using the bamboo mat as a guider, roll the rice and nori away from you, holding the filling in place so that it is enclosed by the rice and nori. Do not enclose the mat! Roll up almost to the top edge of the nori, brush the edge with water, then roll up and seal the edge. Roll the completed sushi firmly again in the mat to give it a good shape. Set aside.

✦ Continue making sushi rolls with the remaining rice and filling ingredients.

✦ Dip a sharp knife into the salted water and cut each roll into 8 neat slices. Turn on end and serve with a variety of dipping sauces.

PER SERVING (4 SLICES OF SUSHI)
227 calories/951 kilojoules; 9 g protein; 0.5 g fat, 2% of calories (0.1 g saturated, 0.4% of calories; 0.1 g monounsaturated, 0.4%; 0.3 g polyunsaturated, 1.2%); 47 g carbohydrate; 1.4 g dietary fiber; 122 mg sodium; 0.5 mg iron; 11 mg cholesterol.

Autumn Rice

AKI NO TAKIKOMI-GOHAN

SERVES 4

2 cups (16 fl oz / 500 ml) dashi
(see page 20)

2½ cups (17½ oz / 550 g)
long-grain rice

5 teaspoons reduced-sodium soy
sauce

3 tablespoons plus 2 teaspoons
sake (rice wine)

8 oz (250 g) small Japanese
black fungi

8 oz (250 g) boneless, skinless
chicken thighs (thigh fillets),
chopped into bite-sized pieces

1 teaspoon peanut oil

2 oz (60 g) tofu

12 canned water chestnuts,
drained and sliced

1 daikon (Japanese radish),
thinly sliced

4 tablespoons chopped perilla or
flat-leaf parsley, optional

perilla or flat-leaf parsley sprigs,
for garnish

Rice is an important staple in the Japanese diet. Uncooked, it is called "kome." Once cooked, it is called "gohan," which also translates to "honorable food." If black fungi are not available, use another Japanese mushroom, such as shiitake.

PREPARATION   *30 minutes plus standing time*

◆ Prepare the dashi in advance.

◆ Rinse the rice under cold running water until the water runs clear.

◆ Place the dashi, rice, 3 teaspoons of the soy sauce and 3 tablespoons of the sake in a large, heavy-bottomed saucepan. Stir well, then let stand for 30 minutes.

◆ Separate the fungi into sprigs of 3 and trim off the roots.

◆ Place the chicken in a small bowl, then add the remaining soy sauce and sake. Mix well. Cover and leave to marinate in the refrigerator for 10 minutes.

◆ Heat the oil in a small, non-stick skillet over medium heat. Add the tofu and cook quickly, until light brown on all sides. Use a slotted spoon to remove the tofu, then slice into cubes.

COOKING   *1 hour*

◆ Add the chicken mixture, water chestnuts and fungi to the rice mixture in the saucepan and mix well. Cover and bring to a boil over medium heat. Increase the heat to high for 30 seconds, then reduce to low-medium and cook for 10 minutes. Reduce the heat again and simmer for 20 minutes.

◆ Place the tofu cubes, daikon and chopped perilla, if using, on top of the rice mixture, increase the heat to high again for 10 seconds. Turn the heat off, place a clean folded cloth between the saucepan and the lid, and leave to stand for 20 minutes.

◆ Stir the rice mixture gently, spoon onto a serving dish and serve, garnished with the perilla sprigs.

PER SERVING

626 calories / 2621 kilojoules; 24 g protein; 7 g fat, 10% of calories (0.5 g saturated, 0.7% of calories; 1 g monounsaturated, 1.4%; 5.5 g polyunsaturated, 7.9%); 112 g carbohydrate; 6.3 g dietary fiber; 377 mg sodium; 1.8 mg iron; 81 mg cholesterol.

An impressive landmark at Wushi in Kiangsu Province.

Autumn Rice

Noodles Nagasaki-Style

NAGASAKI SARA UDON

SERVES 4

4 dried shiitake mushrooms
5 oz (150 g) loin pork (fillet),
    thinly sliced
pinch salt
pinch freshly ground white pepper
8 large raw shrimp (prawns),
    shelled and deveined
1 small squid, cleaned, thinly
    sliced and skinned
2 tablespoons plus 2 teaspoons
    sake (rice wine)
2 tablespoons sesame oil
1 lb (500 g) fresh udon (wheat)
    noodles
1 tablespoon vegetable oil
1 onion, cut into 12 wedges
1 cup (3 oz/90 g) shredded
    Chinese cabbage
12 snow peas (mange-tout)
½ cup (1 oz/30 g) thinly sliced
    canned bamboo shoots
2 cups (4 oz/125 g) bean sprouts
2½ cups (20 fl oz/600 ml)
    reduced-sodium chicken stock,
    skimmed of fat
1 teaspoon finely chopped ginger
1 tablespoon reduced-sodium
    soy sauce
1 tablespoon sugar
1 tablespoon cornstarch (cornflour)
1 tablespoon water
herb sprigs, for garnish

It was through Nagasaki, a busy port in southern Japan, that many Chinese foods were introduced into Japanese cooking. This noodle dish relies on several Chinese ingredients, such as Chinese cabbage, bamboo shoots and bean sprouts.

PREPARATION   *25 minutes*

◆ Soak the shiitake mushrooms in boiling water until soft, about 20 minutes, then drain and slice.
◆ Mix the pork with the salt and pepper.
◆ Mix the shrimp and squid with the 2 teaspoons of sake.

COOKING   *20 minutes*

◆ Heat the sesame oil in a wok or large, heavy-bottomed skillet over medium-high heat. Add the noodles and stir-fry until hot and lightly browned, about 5 minutes. Remove the noodles from the wok and keep hot.
◆ Heat the vegetable oil in the wok. Add the pork and stir-fry until cooked through, about 1 to 2 minutes. Using a slotted spoon, transfer to a plate.
◆ Add the shrimp and squid to the wok and stir-fry until the shrimp turn pink. Using a slotted spoon, transfer to the plate with the pork.
◆ Add the onion to the wok and stir-fry for 1 minute. Add the cabbage, snow peas and shiitake mushrooms and stir-fry for 2 minutes. Add the bamboo shoots, bean sprouts, stock and ginger and bring to a boil, stirring continuously.

◆ Reduce the heat to low, add the remaining sake, the soy sauce, sugar, pork, shrimp and squid and bring to a simmer.
◆ Mix together the cornstarch and water. Add to the wok and stir until thickened.
◆ Divide the hot noodles among 4 large serving bowls and spoon the pork, seafood and vegetable mixture on top. Serve, garnished with the herb sprigs.

PER SERVING
448 calories/1874 kilojoules; 27 g protein; 13 g fat,
27% of calories (1.3 g saturated, 2.7% of calories;
3.7 g monounsaturated, 7.6%; 8 g polyunsaturated, 16.7%);
55 g carbohydrate; 2.2 g dietary fiber; 586 mg sodium;
1.3 mg iron; 101 mg cholesterol.

Cold Noodles in a Basket

HIYASHI SOMEN

SERVES 6

DIPPING SAUCE

1 cup (8 fl oz/250 ml) dashi
   (see page 20)
⅓ cup (3 fl oz/90 ml) Japanese
   soy sauce
⅓ cup (3 fl oz/90 ml) mirin
   (sweet rice wine)
¼ cup (2 fl oz/60 ml) sake
   (rice wine)

2 tablespoons wasabi paste
   (Japanese horseradish)
6 scallions (spring onions), sliced
2 tablespoons chopped pickled
   ginger
1 cup (2 oz/60 g) bean sprouts
   or snow pea (mange-tout)
   sprouts
1 lb (500 g) somen (thin wheat
   noodles)
3 sheets nori (dried seaweed)

During the summer, the Japanese like to eat thin wheat noodles, called *somen*, served cold. They are traditionally served with ice cubes placed on top to chill them and they are presented in a curved bamboo basket so that they can continue to drain.

PREPARATION   *15 minutes plus cooling time*
✦ Combine all the dipping sauce ingredients in a small saucepan and bring to a boil. Reduce the heat and simmer for 5 minutes. Pour into a small bowl and cool to room temperature.
✦ Place the wasabi, scallions, ginger and bean sprouts separately in small bowls.

COOKING   *15 minutes*
✦ Bring a large saucepan of water to a boil. Add the noodles and stir to prevent them from sticking together while the water comes back to a boil. Reduce the heat to medium-high and cook the noodles according to the package directions until tender.
✦ Meanwhile, preheat the broiler (grill).
✦ Drain the noodles in a colander, then run cold water over them until they are cold and drain again.

✦ Toast the sheets of nori under a hot broiler (grill), without turning, until crisp, about 1 minute.
✦ Divide the cold noodles among 6 bamboo baskets or bowls, then crumble the toasted nori over the top of the noodles. Serve with the bowls of dipping sauce and other accompaniments.

PER SERVING
331 calories/1385 kilojoules; 11 g protein; 2.1 g fat, 6% of calories (2.1 g polyunsaturated, 6%); 65 g carbohydrate; 1.1 g dietary fiber; 901 mg sodium; 0.6 mg iron; 0 mg cholesterol.

A basket shop in Kyoto with just a sample of its many different shapes and sizes of basket.

Stuffed Minced Lamb Patties

KIBBI

SERVES 4

1½ cups (8 oz/250 g) bulghur
1 lb (500 g) lean, finely ground
    (minced) lamb
¼ teaspoon ground nutmeg
¼ teaspoon ground cinnamon
½ teaspoon salt
generous pinch cayenne pepper

STUFFING

4 teaspoons virgin olive oil
4 teaspoons pine nuts
4 teaspoons finely chopped onion
4 oz (125 g) lean, finely ground
    (minced) lamb
generous pinch ground allspice
¼ teaspoon salt
freshly ground black pepper,
    to taste

Wheat and rice have been used for centuries in and around Lebanon. Bulghur is made by steaming and drying wheat grains and is a key ingredient in many Lebanese dishes. It is available in health food stores and some supermarkets.

PREPARATION   *20 minutes*

◆ Place the bulghur in a bowl, add enough cold water to cover and let soak for 10 minutes. Drain through a sieve lined with a piece of cheesecloth. Wrap the cheesecloth around the bulghur and squeeze out the excess water.

COOKING   *20 minutes*

◆ Place the bulghur, lamb, nutmeg, cinnamon, salt and cayenne pepper in a large mixing bowl. With clean fingertips, knead the mixture until it is smooth and evenly combined.
◆ Divide the mixture into 8 equal portions. With cold, wet hands, shape each portion into a patty or burger shape, about ½ in (1 cm) thick.
◆ For the stuffing, heat the oil in a medium-sized, non-stick skillet over medium heat. Add the pine nuts and cook until golden, about 3 minutes. Using a slotted spoon, transfer the pine nuts to a plate lined with paper towels and set aside to drain.
◆ Add the onion to the skillet and cook, stirring frequently, until soft and golden, about 5 minutes.
◆ Add the lamb and cook, stirring, until it is no longer pink, about 3 minutes. Remove the skillet from the heat and drain off any visible oil.

◆ Add the pine nuts, allspice, salt and pepper to the skillet with the lamb and onion and combine well. Leave to cool for about 10 minutes.
◆ Divide the stuffing into 8 equal portions and place a portion on each bulghur and lamb patty. With cold, wet hands, mold the patty around the stuffing to make either a patty shape or an egg shape with pointed ends.
◆ Preheat a broiler (grill). Line the broiler pan with aluminum foil. Place the patties in the broiler pan and lightly spray with olive oil cooking spray. Cook about 3 in (8 cm) under the broiler until browned, about 5 minutes. Turn, spray the other side with oil, and cook until the lamb is no longer pink when pierced with a sharp, pointed knife, an additional 5 minutes.
◆ Transfer to a serving platter and serve immediately with a salad and Lebanese pita bread.

PER SERVING
439 calories/1838 kilojoules; 41 g protein; 14 g fat,
28% of calories (4.1 g saturated, 8.1% of calories;
7.1 g monounsaturated, 14.2%; 2.8 g polyunsaturated, 5.7%);
37 g carbohydrate; 10 g dietary fiber; 467 mg sodium; 4.9 mg iron;
103 mg cholesterol.

Bulghur Meatballs

KEFTEDE

SERVES 6

¾ cup (4 oz / 125 g) bulghur
½ cup (4 oz / 125 g) cooked
    chickpeas
1 lb (500 g) lean, finely ground
    (minced) lamb
½ cup finely crumbled pita bread
1 large egg, lightly beaten
¼ cup (2 fl oz / 60 ml) freshly
    squeezed lemon juice
1 garlic clove, crushed
1½ teaspoons ground coriander
1 teaspoon ground cumin
½ teaspoon salt
¼ teaspoon freshly ground white
    pepper
¼ cup chopped mint or flat-leaf
    parsley
3 tablespoons virgin olive oil
mint or parsley sprigs, for
    garnish
salad leaves, for garnish
⅓ cup (3 oz / 90 g) low-fat
    plain yogurt

Bulghur, or cooked cracked wheat, is a great extender and binding agent in these tasty meatballs. It is also a good source of complex carbohydrate and fiber—because it is produced with very little processing, all the goodness is retained.

PREPARATION   *30 minutes*

◆ Place the bulghur in a small bowl, add enough cold water to cover and let soak for 10 minutes. Drain through a sieve lined with a piece of cheesecloth. Wrap the cheesecloth around the bulghur and squeeze out the excess water.

◆ Place the chickpeas in a blender or a food processor fitted with a metal blade and blend until finely chopped.

COOKING   *30 minutes plus chilling time*

◆ Place the bulghur, chickpeas, lamb, bread crumbs, egg, lemon juice, garlic, coriander, cumin, salt, pepper and mint in a large mixing bowl and combine well.

◆ With cold, wet hands, roll the mixture into 30 balls, about 1½ in (3 cm) in diameter. Place on a large plate, cover and refrigerate for at least 20 minutes. Re-roll the chilled meatballs, if necessary, to refine the shape.

◆ Heat half the oil in a large, non-stick skillet over medium heat. Reduce the heat to low, add half the meatballs and cook, moving and turning over frequently, until browned on all sides and cooked in the center, about 6 to 8 minutes. To test, cut a meatball in half; the center should not be pink. Using a slotted spoon, transfer the meatballs to a plate lined with paper towels to drain. Cover with aluminum foil and keep hot.

◆ Heat the remaining oil in the skillet and cook the remaining meatballs in the same manner. Drain well.

◆ Place the meatballs on a warm serving platter. Serve hot, garnished with the mint and salad leaves. Serve the yogurt in a bowl on the side.

PER SERVING

333 calories / 1396 kilojoules; 25 g protein; 12 g fat, 34% of calories (3.1 g saturated, 8.8% of calories; 7.1 g monounsaturated, 20.1%; 1.8 g polyunsaturated, 5.1%); 30 g carbohydrate; 5.4 g dietary fiber; 437 mg sodium; 3.2 mg iron; 85 mg cholesterol.

Bulghur Meatballs

Couscous with Chickpeas and Vegetables

COUSCOUS B'LHUMMUS KHODRA

A vegetarian inspiration—here a spicy, colorful Moroccan vegetable stew is spooned over delicious and easy-to-prepare couscous. The traditional method for cooking couscous is simplified in this recipe.

SERVES 4

½ cup (3½ oz / 110 g) dried
  chickpeas
2 tablespoons virgin olive oil
2 garlic cloves, crushed
1 onion, chopped
1 teaspoon ground cinnamon
1 teaspoon paprika
1 teaspoon ground cumin
2 carrots, sliced
4 baby turnips or baby rutabaga
  (swede)
4 cups (1 lb / 500 g) sweet
  potato, cut into chunks
1 cup (8 fl oz / 250 ml) tomato
  juice
1½ cups (12 fl oz / 375 ml)
  vegetable stock
4 oz (125 g) okra or 3 zucchini
  (courgettes), sliced
¼ cup (1 oz / 30 g) dried apricots
8 button mushrooms
2 tablespoons chopped parsley
salt, to taste
freshly ground black pepper, to
  taste
1 cup (8 fl oz / 250 ml) water
1⅓ cups (8 oz / 250 g) precooked
  couscous
3 tablespoons golden raisins
  (sultanas)
snipped chives, for garnish
yellow rose petals, for garnish,
  optional

PREPARATION   *1 hour plus at least 1 hour soaking time*
✦ Place the chickpeas in a bowl, cover with boiling water and soak for at least 1 hour, or overnight. Drain the chickpeas, place in a large saucepan and cover with fresh water. Cover and bring to a boil. Cook over medium heat until tender, about 1 hour. Drain and set aside.

COOKING   *40 minutes*
✦ Heat 1 tablespoon of the oil in a large, heavy-bottomed saucepan over low-medium heat. Add the garlic, onion, cinnamon, paprika and cumin and cook, stirring occasionally, until the onion is soft, about 3 minutes.
✦ Add the carrots, turnips and sweet potatoes and cook, stirring continuously, for 5 minutes.
✦ Add the tomato juice and stock and bring to a boil. Cover, reduce the heat and simmer for 15 minutes. Add the chickpeas, okra, apricots, mushrooms and parsley and simmer until the vegetables are tender, about 10 minutes. Season to taste with the salt and pepper.

✦ Bring the water to a boil in a large saucepan. Add the couscous and golden sultanas and mix well with a fork. Remove the saucepan from the heat and let stand for 2 minutes to allow the couscous to swell. Add the remaining oil to the center of the couscous, return the saucepan to the heat and cook over medium heat, stirring until heated through, about 4 to 5 minutes.
✦ Spoon the couscous around the edge of a serving dish and garnish with the chives. Spoon the chickpea and vegetable mixture into the center of the couscous and sprinkle with the rose petals, if using. Serve immediately.

PER SERVING
489 calories / 2048 kilojoules; 15 g protein; 9.7 g fat, 18% of calories (1.2 g saturated, 2.2% of calories; 6 g monounsaturated, 11.1%; 2.5 g polyunsaturated, 4.7%); 86 g carbohydrate; 13 g dietary fiber; 217 mg sodium; 7.6 mg iron; 0 mg cholesterol.

A village set in the barren landscape of Morocco.

Couscous with Chickpeas and Vegetables

Couscous with Veal and Vegetables

COUSCOUS DE'AL LHAME KHODRA

SERVES 4

2 lb (1 kg) veal shank (knuckle)
5 cups (40 fl oz / 1.25 l) water
1⅓ cups (8 oz / 250 g) couscous
1 large onion, chopped
2 teaspoons harissa sauce plus
    extra, for serving
½ teaspoon powdered saffron or
    ground turmeric
¼ teaspoon salt
¼ teaspoon freshly ground
    white pepper
4 carrots, cut into 2 in (4 cm)
    lengths
8 oz (250 g) eggplant
    (aubergine), cut into 1 in
    (2 cm) chunks
1 red bell pepper (capsicum),
    seeded and cut into 8
    segments
2 vine-ripened tomatoes, cut into
    wedges
2 tablespoons tomato paste
1 lb (500 g) winter squash
    (pumpkin), cut into 1½ in
    (3 cm) chunks
1 tablespoon butter
1 teaspoon ground cinnamon
parsley sprigs, for garnish

This Moroccan specialty is traditionally cooked in a two-part vessel called a *couscoussier*. The stew simmers in the bottom section and the couscous steams in the top. Alternatively, use a large saucepan and a colander lined with cheesecloth.

PREPARATION   *30 minutes*

✦ With a small, sharp knife, scrape the veal shank clean of any crushed bone particles.
✦ Bring 1 cup of the water to a boil. Place the couscous in a bowl, add the boiling water. Set aside to let the couscous swell, about 15 minutes. Stir the couscous with a fork.

COOKING   *1¼ hours*

✦ Place the veal, onion, the remaining water, the 2 teaspoons of harissa, saffron, salt and pepper in a couscoussier or a large, heavy-bottomed saucepan. Cover and bring to a boil. Reduce the heat and simmer until the veal is tender, about 45 minutes. Remove the veal from the couscoussier.
✦ Raise the heat to medium-high, add the carrots, eggplant, bell pepper, tomatoes, tomato paste and winter squash to the couscoussier. Cover and bring to a boil, then reduce the heat to low.
✦ Remove the lid and place the couscous in the top section of the couscoussier. Cover securely with a lid, or aluminum foil, and steam over the simmering vegetable mixture for 30 minutes, tossing the grains with a fork after 15 minutes.

✦ Meanwhile, cut the veal from the bone and cut into 1 in (2 cm) pieces. Discard the bone.
✦ Transfer the couscous to a warm bowl, add the butter and cinnamon and mix well with a fork.
✦ Add the veal to the vegetables in the couscoussier and heat through.
✦ Pile the couscous in a ring around the edge of a large serving platter and spoon the veal and vegetable stew into the center. Garnish with the parsley sprigs and serve with a bowl with the extra harissa sauce. (A small amount of harissa can also be mixed with some of the liquid from the stew and poured over the couscous for extra spicy flavor.)

PER SERVING
386 calories / 1615 kilojoules; 36 g protein; 5.1 g fat,
12% of calories (2.5 g saturated, 5.9% of calories;
1.2 g monounsaturated, 2.9%; 1.4 g polyunsaturated, 3.2%);
50 g carbohydrate; 7.2 g dietary fiber; 372 mg sodium;
6.6 mg iron; 110 mg cholesterol.

Couscous with Veal and Vegetables

Couscous with Lamb and Quinces

TAJINE DE'AL LHAME S'FARGAL

SERVES 6

½ teaspoon saffron threads
2 cups (16 fl oz/500 ml)
   plus 2 tablespoons water
7 onions
1 tablespoon virgin olive oil
1 teaspoon ground ginger
½ teaspoon freshly ground
   black pepper
½ teaspoon cayenne pepper
2 tablespoons chopped flat-leaf
   parsley
2 lb (1 kg) lean lamb, diced
1½ cups (10 oz/300 g)
   couscous
1 lb (500 g) quinces, peeled,
   cored and sliced
⅓ cup (3 oz/90 g) sugar,
   or to taste
2 tablespoons (1 oz/30 g) butter
½ teaspoon ground cinnamon

The Berbers introduced couscous to North Africa, but Moroccan recipes are acknowledged as the finest of all. The combination of meat and fruit is an ancient feature of this cuisine. Quinces are always served cooked.

PREPARATION   *20 minutes*
◆ Soak the saffron threads in the 2 tablespoons of water for 15 minutes. Then strain, and discard the threads.
◆ Grate 3 of the onions, and chop the remaining onions.

COOKING   *2½ hours*
◆ Heat the oil in the base of a couscoussier over low heat. (If you don't have a couscoussier, use a large, heavy-bottomed saucepan with a cheesecloth-lined steamer or colander.) Add the grated onions, ginger, black pepper, saffron liquid, cayenne pepper and parsley and cook gently for 2 minutes.
◆ Raise the heat to medium-high and add the lamb. Cook, stirring occasionally, until the lamb has changed color but has not browned, about 5 minutes.
◆ Pour in the remaining water and bring to a boil. Lower the heat, cover and simmer for about 1 hour. Check occasionally to make sure that all the water has not evaporated; if necessary, add a little boiling water.
◆ Meanwhile, place the couscous in a large bowl. Cover with cold water, stir once and drain immediately. Stir again once or twice, then let stand until the grains begin to swell, about 15 minutes.

◆ Add the chopped onions to the lamb mixture.
◆ Separate the couscous grains lightly with your fingertips, and tip half the grains into the top section of the couscoussier. Place this over the simmering lamb and leave until steam rises. Then add the remaining couscous. Steam the couscous, uncovered, for about 30 minutes, checking from time to time that all the liquid has not evaporated. Occasionally toss the grains with a fork to prevent lumps from forming.
◆ While the lamb and couscous cook, place the quinces in a medium-sized saucepan, and add just enough water to cover. Add the sugar and simmer over low heat until the quinces are tender, about 15 minutes. Drain.
◆ Remove the top half of the couscoussier from the heat and tip the grains onto a large, shallow platter. Separate the grains with damp fingers. Add the butter to the couscous and rub it in lightly with the palms of your hands, tossing the couscous at the same time.
◆ Add the quinces to the lamb mixture. Replace the top half of the couscoussier and slowly trickle the couscous back into it. Cover and steam for 20 minutes, tossing the grains with a fork from time to time.
◆ Taste the lamb mixture, and adjust the seasoning to taste. You may need to add more sugar.
◆ Place the couscous in a ring around the edge of a large, warm serving dish. Spoon the lamb and quinces into the center and pour the sauce on top. Sprinkle with the cinnamon and serve.

PER SERVING
477 calories/1995 kilojoules; 41 g protein; 13 g fat,
24% of calories (6.2 g saturated, 11.5% of calories;
5.7 g monounsaturated, 10.6%; 1.1 g polyunsaturated, 1.9%);
50 g carbohydrate; 9.3 g dietary fiber; 196 mg sodium;
5.7 mg iron; 120 mg cholesterol.

Many rural Moroccans still use the traditional beasts of burden.

Barcelona Paella

ARROZ BARCELONES

SERVES 8

1 Spanish chorizo sausage,
about 6½ oz (200 g)
1 large red bell pepper (capsicum)
1 green or yellow bell pepper
(capsicum)
4 teaspoons virgin olive oil
4 oz (125 g) thickly sliced
pancetta, cut in julienne strips
8 oz (250 g) pork loin (fillet),
diced
3 garlic cloves, crushed
2½ lb (1.25 kg) vine-ripened
tomatoes, peeled and chopped
3 cups (2 lb 5 oz/660 g)
short-grain rice
2 cups (10 oz/300 g) peas
½ teaspoon paprika
½ teaspoon salt
6 cups (48 fl oz/1.5 l) chicken
stock, skimmed of fat
½ teaspoon saffron threads
½ cup (2 oz/60 g) freshly grated
Parmesan cheese

This rice dish is a speciality of Barcelona. The paella is finished with a sprinkle of freshly grated cheese, then briefly baked for serving. This unusual feature is probably a legacy from the time when Milan was part of the Spanish empire.

PREPARATION   *20 minutes*
✦ Remove the casing from the chorizo sausage and crumble it.
✦ Core and seed the bell peppers and slice thinly lengthwise.

COOKING   *1 hour*
✦ Heat 2 teaspoons of the oil in a paella pan or large, flameproof casserole dish over low heat. Add the pancetta and cook for 2 minutes.
✦ Add the chorizo and pork and cook, stirring occasionally, until the pork is no longer pink, about 5 minutes. Using a slotted spoon, transfer to a plate.
✦ Add the bell peppers to the pan and cook, stirring frequently, until they are soft, about 5 minutes. Transfer to the plate with the meats.
✦ Preheat the oven to 350°F (180°C).
✦ Add the remaining oil, the garlic and tomatoes to the pan, and cook, stirring frequently, over medium heat, for 10 minutes.

✦ Stir in the rice, peas, pancetta, chorizo, pork, bell peppers, paprika and salt.
✦ Meanwhile, bring the chicken stock to a boil in a medium-sized saucepan. Stir the saffron into the boiling stock and add to the pan with the rice mixture. Bring to a boil, stirring continuously. Cover, reduce the heat to medium and cook for 10 minutes.
✦ Remove from the heat and sprinkle the cheese on the top.
✦ Bake until the rice is tender, about 10 minutes. Let stand in a warm place for 5 minutes before serving.

PER SERVING
*603 calories/2525 kilojoules; 25 g protein; 22 g fat,
33% of calories (8.8 g saturated, 13.2% of calories;
10.5 g monounsaturated, 15.8%; 2.7 g polyunsaturated, 4%);
74 g carbohydrate; 6.9 g dietary fiber; 976 mg sodium;
2.5 mg iron; 109 mg cholesterol.*

Rice with Smoked Trout and Artichokes

ARROZ CON TRUCHAS AHUMADO Y ALCACHOFAS

SERVES 6

2 cups (14 oz/440 g) short-
grain rice
¼ teaspoon powdered saffron
1 tablespoon warm water
1 tablespoon virgin olive oil
2 garlic cloves, crushed
2 vine-ripened tomatoes, chopped
4 cups (32 fl oz/1 l) water
1 cup (5 oz/150 g) peas
1 cup (5 oz/150 g) sliced
green beans
8 oz (250 g) smoked trout
5½ oz (170 g) pickled artichoke
hearts, drained
½ cup (2 oz/60 g) sundried
tomatoes packed in oil,
drained and sliced

This is a lighter, more elegant version of *Arroz con Bacalao y Alcachofas,* a dish traditionally made with smoked cod. Like other recipes from the area around Valencia, it includes plenty of vegetables.

PREPARATION   *15 minutes*
✦ Wash the rice under cold running water until the water runs clear. Drain.
✦ Dissolve the saffron in the warm water.

COOKING   *30 minutes*
✦ Heat the oil in a large, heavy-bottomed saucepan over medium heat. Add the garlic and cook until golden, about 2 minutes. Add the tomatoes and cook, stirring occasionally, for 3 minutes.
✦ Add the water, cover and bring to a boil. Add the rice and saffron liquid, stirring well with a wooden spoon. Return to a boil and cook, uncovered, for 5 minutes.

✦ Add the peas and beans and cook, stirring frequently, until the rice is tender, about 5 minutes.
✦ While the rice is cooking, remove the skin and any bones from the smoked trout and, with a fork, flake the flesh into large pieces.
✦ Gently fold the trout, artichokes and sundried tomatoes into the rice mixture and cook over low heat until heated through. Transfer to a serving platter and serve, accompanied by a green salad.

PER SERVING
*395 calories/1653 kilojoules; 19 g protein; 5.9 g fat, 14% of
calories (1.1 g saturated, 2.5% of calories; 3.1 g monounsaturated,
7.4%; 1.7 g polyunsaturated, 4.1%); 66 g carbohydrate;
4.9 g dietary fiber; 162 mg sodium; 1.7 mg iron; 33 mg cholesterol.*

Paella

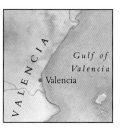

SERVES 6

12 jumbo (large) raw shrimp
    (prawns)
1 chicken, about 3 lb (1.5 kg)
1 tablespoon virgin olive oil
1 Spanish chorizo sausage,
    about 6½ oz (200 g),
    thickly sliced
8 oz (250 g) lean cooked ham,
    cubed
1 large red onion, chopped
2 garlic cloves, crushed
2 vine-ripened tomatoes,
    chopped
2 teaspoons tomato paste
1 cup (8 fl oz/250 ml) dry
    white wine
1 teaspoon saffron threads
2 cups (14 oz/440 g) short-
    grain rice
3 cups (24 fl oz/750 ml)
    chicken stock, skimmed of fat
6 mussels, or 12 clams, in the
    shell, scrubbed and debearded
1 small red bell pepper
    (capsicum), seeded and sliced
1 cup (4 oz/125 g) peas
1 lb (500 g) cooked lobster tail
    in the shell, thickly sliced,
    optional
2 tablespoons chopped parsley
1 lemon, cut into wedges,
    for garnish
chopped herbs, for garnish

Paella was originally cooked on an open fire in a large flat pan called a *paellera*.
When it was first made, in Valencia, only two or three ingredients were added to
the rice. Today a paella may include a variety of meats, vegetables and seafood,
and each region of Spain has its own version.

PREPARATION   *30 minutes*

✦ Peel and devein the shrimp, leaving the tail shell
attached.
✦ Cut the chicken into serving pieces. Remove and
discard the backbone and as much skin as possible.

COOKING   *1 hour*

✦ Heat the oil in a paella pan or large, flameproof
casserole dish over medium heat. Add the chicken
pieces, chorizo and ham and cook, turning and
stirring frequently, until the chicken is sealed and
golden, about 8 to 10 minutes. Using a slotted spoon,
transfer the chicken, chorizo and ham to a plate.
✦ Add the shrimp to the pan and cook, stirring frequently, until the shrimp change to an orange color,
about 4 minutes. Using a slotted spoon, transfer the
shrimp to a plate.
✦ Preheat the oven to 350°F (180°C).
✦ Add the onion and garlic to the pan and cook,
stirring occasionally, until the onion is soft, about 3
minutes.
✦ Reduce the heat to low, add the tomatoes and tomato paste to the pan and simmer for 5 minutes.

✦ Meanwhile, heat ¼ cup of the wine in a small saucepan over low heat. Pour the wine into a small bowl
and add the saffron threads. Let soak for 4 minutes,
strain, and add the saffron liquid to the pan with the
onion and tomato mixture.
✦ Add the rice, stock and the remaining wine. Bring
to a boil, stirring continuously, then remove from the
heat.
✦ Arrange the chicken, chorizo, ham, mussels and red
pepper slices over the rice and sprinkle the peas on top.
Cover the pan securely with a lid or aluminum foil.
✦ Bake until the rice is tender, about 30 minutes. Without stirring, place the shrimp and lobster, if using, on
top of the mixture and bake, uncovered, for an additional 5 minutes. Discard any unopened mussels.
Sprinkle with the parsley and serve immediately, garnished with the lemon wedges and chopped herbs.

PER SERVING
*682 calories/2855 kilojoules; 64 g protein; 17 g fat, 23% of
calories (5.4 g saturated, 7.6% of calories; 8.2 g monounsaturated,
11.2%; 3.4 g polyunsaturated, 4.2%); 59 g carbohydrate;
4.9 g dietary fiber; 1467 mg sodium; 4.6 mg iron;
239 mg cholesterol.*

*A cobbled
laneway sets a
tranquil scene
in a village on
the island of
Majorca.*

Paella

Rice and Fish "Served Apart"

ARROZ ABANDA

Gulf of
Valencia
Valencia
VALENCIA

SERVES 4

1 lb (500 g) mussels in the shell
12 jumbo (large) raw shrimp
    (prawns)
4 oz (125 g) squid, thinly sliced
1 lb (500 g) firm white fish, cut
    into large cubes
4 cups (32 fl oz/1 l) water
2 cups (16 fl oz/500 ml) dry
    white wine
1 teaspoon salt
2 bay leaves
½ teaspoon peppercorns
2 fennel sprigs plus extra
    for garnish
¼ cup (1 oz/30 g) ground
    almonds
grated zest and juice of 1 orange
¼ cup (2 fl oz/60 ml) dry sherry
12 saffron threads
2 tablespoons virgin olive oil
4 garlic cloves, crushed
1 white onion, finely chopped
2 vine-ripened tomatoes, chopped
½ teaspoon fennel seeds
1½ cups (10½ oz/330 g)
    short-grain rice
lemon wedges, for serving
garlic-flavored mayonnaise or
    plain yogurt, for serving

In this classic dish from Valencia, the saffron rice and the seafood are served
"abanda" or "apart." The rice is served as a first course and the seafood is served
as the main course. The region's coastal waters abound with excellent seafood.

PREPARATION   *20 minutes*
◆ Scrub and debeard the mussels.
◆ Devein the shrimp, but leave the shell segments at-
tached, if possible.

COOKING   *45 minutes*
◆ Place the mussels, squid, fish and shrimp together
with the water, wine, salt, bay leaves, peppercorns and
fennel in a large, heavy-bottomed saucepan. Cover and
bring to a boil, then reduce the heat and simmer until the mussels have opened and the shrimp have turned
pink, about 8 to 10 minutes. Discard any unopened
mussels.
◆ Strain the seafood and reserve the liquid. Place the
seafood on a warm serving dish, then sprinkle on the
almonds and orange zest followed by the orange juice
and 2 tablespoons of the sherry. Cover with aluminum
foil and keep warm.
◆ Mix the saffron with 1 tablespoon of the reserved fish
liquid.
◆ Heat the oil in a medium-sized, heavy-bottomed
saucepan over low heat. Add the garlic and onion and
cook until the onion is soft, about 3 minutes.
◆ Strain the saffron liquid and add the liquid, tomatoes
and fennel to the garlic and onion. Raise the heat to
medium and cook, stirring frequently, for 2 minutes.

◆ Add the rice and stir until the grains are evenly
coated with the mixture, about 1 minute. Add enough
of the reserved seafood liquid to cover the rice by
1 in (2 cm), adding water if necessary. Bring to a boil,
then cover and reduce the heat to low. Simmer until
the rice is cooked, about 30 minutes.
◆ Stir the remaining sherry into the rice mixture and
spoon into a serving bowl. Garnish both the rice and
the seafood with the fennel sprigs.
◆ Serve the rice for a first course and follow with the
seafood for the main course. Serve the seafood with
the lemon wedges and garlic-flavored mayonnaise or
plain yogurt.

PER SERVING (WITHOUT MAYONNAISE OR YOGURT)
*797 calories/3338 kilojoules; 74 g protein; 14 g fat, 16% of
calories (1.8 g saturated, 2.1% of calories; 8.1 g monounsaturated,
9.3%; 4.1 g polyunsaturated, 4.6%); 67 g carbohydrate;
4.6 g dietary fiber; 1281 mg sodium; 7.7 mg iron;
430 mg cholesterol.*

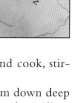

Santander
• Bilbao
VASCONGADAS
Pamplona •
Logroño •
NAVARRA

Fish Paella

PAELLA MARINERA

SERVES 8

1 lb (500 g) squid, cleaned
8 clams
8 mussels
¼ cup (2 fl oz/60 ml) virgin
  olive oil
8 small fresh sardines, gutted
  and boned, optional
2 lb (1 kg) red onions, finely
  chopped
2½ lb (1.25 kg) vine-ripened
  tomatoes, peeled, seeded and
  chopped
4 cups (32 fl oz/1 l) fish or
  vegetable stock
2 garlic cloves, crushed
½ teaspoon saffron threads
¼ cup chopped flat-leaf parsley
1½ cups (10½ oz/330 g)
  short-grain rice
½ teaspoon salt
½ teaspoon freshly ground
  white pepper
18 jumbo (large) cooked shrimp
  (prawns)
8 oz (250 g) scallops
lemon wedges, for serving
½ cup (4 oz/125 g) garlic-
  flavored mayonnaise, optional

This is a fisherman's rice and seafood casserole. It is a very tasty dish, highlighted with the flavor of tomatoes and red onions, and traditionally served with garlic-flavored mayonnaise. For a low-fat dish, omit the mayonnaise.

PREPARATION   *30 minutes*
◆ Cut the squid into thin rings.
◆ Scrub and debeard the clams and the mussels.

COOKING   *1 hour*
◆ Heat 2 tablespoons of the oil in a large, non-stick skillet over medium heat. Reduce the heat to low, add the squid and sardines, if using, and simmer, stirring occasionally, for 3 minutes. Transfer the squid and sardines to separate plates, cover and set aside.
◆ Heat the remaining oil in a paella pan or a large, flameproof casserole dish over low heat. Add the onions and cook, stirring occasionally, until golden, about 5 minutes. Add the tomatoes, increase the heat to medium and cook, stirring frequently, until the tomato juices are slightly reduced, about 10 minutes.
◆ Preheat the oven to 350°F (180°C).
◆ Bring the stock to a boil in a medium-sized saucepan over medium heat.
◆ Add the garlic, saffron, parsley, rice, squid, salt and pepper to the paella pan with the onion and tomato mixture and stir well. Add the boiling stock and stir

again. Reduce the heat to low, cover and cook, stirring occasionally, for 10 minutes.
◆ Add the shrimp and scallops, push them down deep into the rice mixture to cover them. Place the sardines on top.
◆ Bake until the rice is tender, about 10 minutes.
◆ Meanwhile, place the clams and mussels in a steamer over a saucepan of boiling water. Cover and steam until the shellfish open, between 5 and 10 minutes. Discard any that do not open. Remove the meat from the shells.
◆ Arrange the mussels and clams on top of the paella. Serve with the lemon wedges for squeezing over the paella. If using, place a tablespoonful of the garlic-flavored mayonnaise on each portion.

PER SERVING (WITHOUT MAYONNAISE)
418 calories/1748 kilojoules; 35 g protein; 12 g fat, 26% of calories (2.7 g saturated, 6% of calories; 6.9 g monounsaturated, 15%; 2.4 g polyunsaturated, 5%); 42 g carbohydrate; 5.2 g dietary fiber; 665 mg sodium; 4.8 mg iron; 240 mg cholesterol.

*A fishing boat
returning to
its home port
on Ibiza.*

Fish Paella

Stir-Fried Thai Noodles
PAHT THAI

SERVES 4

*8 oz (250 g) dried rice noodles
   (about ¼ in/0.5 cm wide)*
½ cup (3 oz/90 g) tofu
10 small dried shrimp (prawns)
3 tablespoons vegetable oil
3 garlic cloves, finely chopped
*8 jumbo (large) raw shrimp
   (prawns), shelled and deveined*
2 large eggs
3 tablespoons lemon juice
3 tablespoons fish sauce
2 tablespoons palm or brown sugar
2 teaspoons sweet paprika
*2 scallions (spring onions),
   cut into 2 in (5 cm) pieces*
2 cups (4 oz/125 g) bean sprouts
*¼ cup (1½ oz/45 g) roasted
   peanuts, chopped*
*cilantro (coriander) sprigs,
   for garnish*

This classic noodle dish is served throughout Thailand, and it is generally eaten as a lunch or as part of a light meal. However, the colorful street stalls, especially in Bangkok, serve it at all hours.

PREPARATION   *15 minutes plus 5 minutes soaking time*
✦ Cover the dried noodles with warm water and soak for 5 minutes, or until softened. Drain well.
✦ Cut the tofu into ¼ in (0.5 cm) cubes.
✦ Finely chop the small dried shrimp.

COOKING   *20 minutes*
✦ Heat the oil in a wok or large skillet over medium-high heat. Add the garlic and stir-fry until just golden, about 20 seconds. Add the raw shrimp and stir-fry until just pink, about 3 minutes. Add the tofu and cook, stirring constantly but gently, for about 3 minutes.
✦ Push the shrimp and tofu mixture to one side, add 1 egg and cook, stirring constantly, for about 1 minute, breaking the egg into pieces. Push the egg pieces to

the side and repeat the process with the second egg.
✦ Add the noodles, dried shrimp, lemon juice, fish sauce, sugar and paprika. Reduce the heat and cook, stirring continuously, until well combined and hot, about 2 minutes. Add the scallions and bean sprouts and cook, stirring continuously, for 2 to 3 minutes.
✦ Spoon the mixture onto a serving dish and sprinkle with the peanuts. Garnish with the cilantro and serve.

PER SERVING
545 calories/2281 kilojoules; 20 g protein; 23 g fat, 38% of calories (4.1 g saturated, 7% of calories; 6.7 g monounsaturated, 11%; 12.2 g polyunsaturated, 20%); 63 g carbohydrate; 2.4 g dietary fiber; 427 mg sodium; 3.1 mg iron; 149 mg cholesterol.

Noodles in Coconut Sauce
MEE GA-THI

SERVES 8

*1 lb (500 g) rice noodles
   (rice vermicelli)*
3 small, well-shaped red chilies
8 oz (250 g) pork loin (fillet)
1 tablespoon vegetable oil
4 scallions (spring onions)
3 oz (90 g) tofu
*1 teaspoon finely chopped
   galangal or ginger*
1 large tomato, cut into wedges
*1 lb (500 g) small raw shrimp
   (prawns), shelled and deveined*
¼ cup (1¼ oz/45 g) brown sugar
*3 cups (24 fl oz/750 ml)
   coconut milk*
*¼ cup (2 fl oz/60 ml) soybean
   paste*
2 tablespoons fish sauce
4 cups (8 oz/250 g) bean sprouts
¼ cup chopped cilantro (coriander)
*¼ cup (¾ oz/20 g) toasted
   shredded coconut*

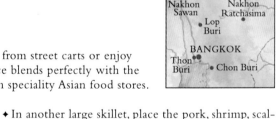

In Thailand, people snack on this delicious noodle dish from street carts or enjoy it at home as a meal. The rich and creamy coconut sauce blends perfectly with the simply prepared noodles. Soybean paste is available from speciality Asian food stores.

PREPARATION   *15 minutes plus 30 minutes soaking time*
✦ Place the noodles in a bowl, add enough cold water to cover and leave to stand for 30 minutes. Drain.
✦ Meanwhile, thinly slice 2 of the chilies. Use a very sharp knife to make 2 or 3 cuts from the pointed end almost to the base of the remaining chili. Place in a bowl of iced water until the "petals" curl, at least 30 minutes.
✦ Thinly slice the pork loin.
✦ Diagonally slice the scallions.
✦ Cut the tofu into ½ in (1 cm) cubes.

COOKING   *10 to 15 minutes*
✦ Heat the oil in a large, heavy-bottomed skillet over medium-high heat. Add the sliced chilies, galangal and tomato and cook for 3 minutes.
✦ Add the drained noodles and stir-fry until the noodles are hot and soft, about 5 minutes.

✦ In another large skillet, place the pork, shrimp, scallions, sugar, coconut milk, soybean paste, fish sauce and bean sprouts. Bring to a boil, then reduce the heat and simmer for 5 minutes. Stir the tofu in gently.
✦ Serve the hot noodle mixture in a warm serving bowl and spoon the coconut milk mixture on top. Sprinkle with the cilantro and toasted coconut and garnish with the chili "flower."

PER SERVING
607 calories/2543 kilojoules; 30 g protein; 23 g fat, 34% of calories (18.3 g saturated, 27.2% of calories; 2.7 g monounsaturated, 4.1%; 2 g polyunsaturated, 2.7%); 70 g carbohydrate; 1.8 g dietary fiber; 632 mg sodium; 3 mg iron; 147 mg cholesterol.

Stir-Fried Thai Noodles

Stir-Fried Rice with Pork

KHAO PAHT MOO

SERVES 4

3 cups (24 fl oz/750 ml) water
pinch salt
1 cup (7 oz/220 g) jasmine or
   other long-grain rice
1 small, well-shaped red chili,
   for chili flower
2 tablespoons vegetable oil
1 onion, chopped
2 garlic cloves, crushed
1 teaspoon ground turmeric
8 oz (250 g) pork loin (fillet),
   thinly sliced
1 tablespoon thinly sliced
   lemongrass
1 teaspoon finely chopped ginger
1 teaspoon finely chopped red chili
2 tablespoons reduced-sodium
   soy sauce
1 cup (8 oz/250 g) sliced
   green beans
8 scallions (spring onions)
½ cup (1½ oz/50 g)
   unsweetened, shredded coconut
1 cup (2 oz/60 g) bean sprouts
2 tablespoons chopped cilantro
   (coriander)
cilantro (coriander) leaves,
   for garnish
8 lime wedges, for serving

A well-balanced Thai meal always contains rice, often accompanied by soup, curry, a fish dish and a salad. This rice dish, flavored with fragrant herbs and spices, combines crunchy vegetables and pork and is a light meal in itself.

PREPARATION   *30 minutes plus 2 hours chilling time*
✦ Place the water in a large, heavy-bottomed saucepan, add the salt and bring to a boil. Add the rice and stir well. Boil for 10 minutes. Drain the rice, rinse under cold, running water, and drain again. Cover and refrigerate for at least 2 hours, or preferably overnight.
✦ Use a very sharp knife to make 2 or 3 cuts from the pointed end of the chili almost to the base of the stem end. Place in a bowl of iced water until the "petals" curl, at least 30 minutes.

COOKING   *15 minutes*
✦ Heat the oil in a wok or large skillet over medium-high heat. Add the onion, garlic and turmeric and stir-fry for 2 minutes.
✦ Add the pork and stir-fry until browned, about 2 minutes. Add the lemongrass, ginger and chopped chili and stir-fry for 1 minute.

✦ Reduce the heat to medium and add the rice, soy sauce and green beans. Cook, stirring continuously, until the rice is heated through, about 5 minutes.
✦ Add the scallions, coconut, bean sprouts and chopped cilantro and toss together until well combined.
✦ Serve immediately in a large, warm bowl, garnished with the chili "flower" and the cilantro leaves. Serve with the lime wedges to squeeze over the rice.

PER SERVING
447 calories/1870 kilojoules; 23 g protein; 17 g fat, 35% of calories (8.7 g saturated, 17.8% of calories; 2.4 g monounsaturated, 4.9 %; 5.9 g polyunsaturated, 12.3 %); 50 g carbohydrate; 7.4 g dietary fiber; 549 mg sodium; 2.6 mg iron; 31 mg cholesterol.

Stir-Fried Rice with Pork

Chiang Mai

Lampang

Phitsanulok

Moulmein

Noodles with Spicy Meat Sauce
KHANOM JEEN NAM NGIOW

SERVES 4

13 oz (410 g) pork loin (fillet)
1 tablespoon vegetable oil
¼ cup (2 oz/60 g) red curry paste
2 tablespoons soybean paste
1 large, vine-ripened tomato,
    chopped
¼ cup (2 fl oz/60 ml) fish sauce
1 tablespoon lime juice
6 kaffir lime or lime leaves,
    fresh or dried
2 cups (16 fl oz/500 ml) water
4 oz (250 g) fresh egg noodles
2 scallions (spring onions),
    thinly sliced diagonally
1 cup (2 oz/60 g) bean sprouts
¼ cup pickled ginger

This curry uses bottled red curry paste, which is readily available in many large supermarkets and in Asian stores. The fiery full flavor of the paste can be attributed to one of its main ingredients: dried red chilies.

PREPARATION   *20 minutes*
✦ Cut the pork into ¾ in (2 cm) cubes.

COOKING   *25 minutes*
✦ Heat the oil in a large, heavy-bottomed saucepan over medium heat. Add the curry paste and cook, stirring continuously, for 3 minutes.
✦ Add the pork and soybean paste and cook, stirring frequently, for 3 minutes.
✦ Add the tomato, fish sauce, lime juice, kaffir lime leaves and water. Bring to a boil, reduce the heat, cover and simmer until the pork is tender, about 15 minutes.
✦ Meanwhile, bring a medium-sized saucepan of water to a boil. Add the noodles and cook until just tender, about 30 seconds. Drain.

✦ Divide the noodles among 4 bowls and spoon the pork curry on top. Sprinkle a quarter of the scallions on top.
✦ Sprinkle some of the bean sprouts and pickled ginger on top of each portion, reserving a little of each to serve in a separate bowl.

PER SERVING
449 calories/1881 kilojoules; 37 g protein; 11 g fat, 22% of calories (2.4 g saturated, 4.9% of calories; 2.9 g monounsaturated, 5.7%; 5.7 g polyunsaturated, 11.4%); 50 g carbohydrate; 3.2 g dietary fiber; 622 mg sodium; 3.8 mg iron; 60 mg cholesterol.

A typical Thai market with a multitude of spices, dried foods and fish among the goods available.

*Noodles with
Spicy Meat Sauce*

Dirty Rice

SERVES 4

1¼ cups (8½ oz/275 g) long-
   grain rice
8 oz (250 g) chicken livers
1 tablespoon vegetable oil
8 oz (250 g) red onions,
   finely chopped
1 garlic clove, crushed
1½ cups thinly sliced scallions
   (spring onions)
1 small red bell pepper
   (capsicum), seeded and cut
   into short strips
1 red chili, seeded and finely
   chopped
2 tablespoons chopped parsley
¼ teaspoon salt
1 cup (8 fl oz/250 ml) chicken
   stock, skimmed of fat

This famous Creole dish from Louisiana is called "dirty rice" because of the dark color of the browned ingredients. Creole cuisine has evolved from myriad influences, including French, Spanish, English, African and Native American. Full-flavored nourishing dishes like this one are typical of its style.

PREPARATION   *20 minutes*

♦ Bring a large saucepan of water to a boil. Add the rice and cook until tender, about 10 to 12 minutes. Drain and rinse under hot running water to remove excess starch. Cover and keep warm.
♦ Cut the chicken livers into ½ in (1 cm) cubes.

COOKING   *20 minutes*

♦ Heat the oil in a large, heavy-bottomed skillet over medium heat. Add the onions and garlic and cook gently, stirring continuously, for 5 minutes.
♦ Add the chicken livers and cook, stirring frequently, until they change color, about 8 minutes.
♦ Add the scallions, bell pepper, chili and parsley and

stir for 2 minutes. Add the salt and mix well.
♦ Place the stock and rice in a large, heavy-bottomed saucepan. Add the chicken liver mixture and stir to mix. Cook over low heat, stirring continuously, until the mixture is heated through, about 5 minutes.
♦ Serve immediately on a warm serving platter, accompanied by a green salad and warm crusty French bread.

PER SERVING

393 calories/1644 kilojoules; 20 g protein; 8.8 g fat, 20% of calories (2.4 g saturated, 5.2% of calories; 2.2 g monounsaturated, 4.6%; 4.2 g polyunsaturated, 10.2%); 58 g carbohydrate; 4.0 g dietary fiber; 534 mg sodium; 7.4 mg iron; 238 mg cholesterol.

Baked Macaroni and Cheese

SERVES 4

1 leek or white onion
1¼ cups (6½ oz/200 g) elbow
   macaroni
2 tablespoons (1 oz/30 g) butter
   or margarine
3 tablespoons (1 oz/30 g) all-
   purpose (plain) flour
2 cups (16 fl oz/500 ml) skim
   milk
¼ cup (2 fl oz/60 ml) dry white
   wine
2 teaspoons whole-grain mustard
½ cup (2 oz/60 g) freshly grated
   reduced-fat cheddar cheese
½ cup (2 oz/60 g) freshly grated
   Swiss cheese
freshly ground black pepper,
   to taste
¼ cup (1 oz/30 g) freshly grated
   Parmesan cheese
¼ cup (¼ oz/10 g) fresh bread
   crumbs

This update of an old favorite features three types of cheese, white wine and leek. To add more color, try substituting vegetable pastas, such as beet or spinach, for the plain macaroni. If you prefer, you can substitute goat cheese, ricotta cheese or mozzarella for one of the cheeses in this recipe.

PREPARATION   *10 minutes*

♦ Wash the leek and cut into ½ in (1 cm) lengths, or cut the onion into 12 wedges.
♦ Preheat the oven to 350°F (180°C).
♦ Spray a shallow 7½ × 10½ in (16 × 26 cm) baking dish with olive oil cooking spray.

COOKING   *30 minutes*

♦ Bring a large saucepan of water to a boil. Add the macaroni and the leek and return to a boil, stirring. Boil rapidly, uncovered, until the macaroni is just tender, about 10 minutes. Reserve ¼ cup (2 fl oz/60 ml) of the macaroni water, then drain the macaroni mixture. Cover and keep warm.
♦ Melt the butter in a large saucepan over medium heat. Add the flour and stir continuously with a wooden spoon until the mixture looks grainy in texture, about 1 minute.

♦ Add the milk, wine and the reserved macaroni water and bring to a boil, stirring continuously.
♦ Reduce the heat to low. Add the mustard and cheddar and Swiss cheeses, and stir until the cheeses have melted. Season to taste with the pepper.
♦ Place the macaroni mixture in the prepared baking dish. Pour the cheese sauce over it and sprinkle with the Parmesan cheese and bread crumbs.
♦ Bake until the Parmesan cheese is golden brown and bubbling hot, about 10 minutes.
♦ Serve immediately with grilled tomatoes or a mixed salad.

PER SERVING

464 calories/1943 kilojoules; 23 g protein; 18 g fat, 35% of calories (9 g saturated, 18.2% of calories; 5.2 g monounsaturated, 9.8%; 3.8 g polyunsaturated, 7%); 50 g carbohydrate; 3.6 g dietary fiber; 406 mg sodium; 0.9 mg iron; 36 mg cholesterol.

Dirty Rice

Quinoa with Red Peppers

High-protein quinoa is very easy to prepare and is a good background for tasty sauces like this one. Quinoa is commonly grouped with grains although it is actually a member of the spinach family. This dish makes an excellent vegetarian meal served with warm cornbread and a green salad.

SERVES 4

3 red bell peppers (capsicum)
1 cup (6 oz/180 g) quinoa
1 tablespoon virgin olive oil
1 white onion, cut into 12 wedges
2 garlic cloves, finely chopped
1 large, vine-ripened tomato, cut
   into 12 wedges
¼ cup (1¼ oz/45 g) black
   olives, pitted and sliced
2 tablespoons capers
1 tablespoon chopped oregano
¼ teaspoon salt
1 tablespoon balsamic vinegar
oregano sprigs, for garnish

PREPARATION   *30 minutes*
✦ Preheat the broiler (grill).
✦ Cut the peppers into wedges, following the natural indentations. Remove the seeds and white membrane. Place, skin side up, under the hot broiler and heat until the skin bubbles and starts to scorch. Place the peppers in a clean plastic bag, seal and cover with a cloth for 5 minutes. Remove the skin from the peppers with your fingers, then cut into long, thin strips.

COOKING   *10 to 12 minutes*
✦ Cook the quinoa according to package directions. Keep hot.
✦ Heat the oil in a large, heavy-bottomed saucepan over low-medium heat. Add the onion and garlic and cook, stirring frequently, for 3 minutes.

✦ Add the tomato and cook, stirring, for 1 minute. Stir in the peppers and heat through, about 2 minutes.
✦ Add the olives, capers, oregano and salt and cook, stirring, for 30 seconds. Add the vinegar, then remove from the heat.
✦ Spoon the quinoa onto a warm serving platter, spoon the pepper mixture into the center, garnish with the oregano sprigs and serve immediately.

PER SERVING
268 calories/1123 kilojoules; 9 g protein; 3.4 g fat; 29% of calories (0.5 g saturated, 4.9% of calories; 2.6 g monounsaturated, 21.2%; 0.3 g polyunsaturated, 2.9%); 39 g carbohydrate; 6.3 g dietary fiber; 425 mg sodium; 0.5 mg iron; 0 mg cholesterol.

Penne with Asparagus and Pecans

Red pesto is a bold variation of the classic Italian basil pesto sauce. Asparagus add freshness and the pecans are a good source of vegetable protein. Spoon the red pesto over the penne for a delicious well-balanced meal. During the summer, serve this dish with a fresh green salad.

SERVES 4

½ cup dry sundried tomatoes
   (not packed in oil)
½ cup sundried tomatoes packed
   in oil
8–10 asparagus spears,
   (about 8 oz/250 g), trimmed
2½ cups (12½ oz/390 g) penne
1 onion, finely chopped
2 garlic cloves, crushed
¼ cup (1 oz/30 g) pecans
½ cup (2 oz/60 g) freshly grated
   Parmesan cheese
2 tablespoons shredded basil
basil sprigs, for garnish

PREPARATION   *20 minutes*
✦ Place the dry sundried tomatoes in a bowl, cover with boiling water and let stand for 10 minutes, then drain.
✦ Drain the sundried tomatoes packed in oil, reserving 1 tablespoon of the oil.
✦ Cut the asparagus spears into quarters.

COOKING   *20 minutes*
✦ Bring a large saucepan of water to a boil. Add the penne and cook until just tender, about 10 minutes. Reserve ½ cup (4 fl oz/125 ml) of the pasta cooking water, then drain.
✦ While the penne is cooking, heat the reserved oil in a small, heavy-bottomed saucepan over low heat. Add the onion and garlic and cook for 5 minutes.
✦ Place all of the sundried tomatoes in the bowl of a food processor or a blender. Process to form a paste.

✦ Add the onion and garlic mixture and the pecans and process to a thick purée. Add the reserved pasta water and Parmesan cheese and mix well.
✦ Cook the asparagus in a steamer over boiling water until tender, about 6 minutes, or place in a clean plastic bag, twist to seal and microwave on High for 2 minutes.
✦ To serve, divide the penne among 4 warm pasta bowls. Top each with the red pesto sauce, then place the asparagus and shredded basil on top. Garnish with the basil sprigs and serve immediately.

PER SERVING
569 calories/2380 kilojoules; 22 g protein; 15 g fat; 27% of calories (4.2 g saturated, 7.6% of calories; 4.9 g monounsaturated, 8.6%; 5.9 g polyunsaturated, 10.8%); 82 g carbohydrate; 7.2 g dietary fiber; 292 mg sodium; 1.9 mg iron; 14 mg cholesterol.

Quinoa with Red Peppers

Duck Congee

CHAO VIT

*1 cup (7 oz/220 g) jasmine or
    other long-grain rice
1 duck, about 4 lb (2 kg),
    cut in half
2 in (5 cm) ginger
1 teaspoon salt
1 tablespoon vegetable oil
1 large onion, quartered
2 garlic cloves, crushed
1 tablespoon palm or brown sugar
4 scallions (spring onions),
    thinly sliced
4 Vietnamese or regular mint
    sprigs, shredded*

GINGER SAUCE

*4 teaspoons finely grated ginger
1 tablespoon brown sugar
2 tablespoons rice vinegar or
    mirin (sweet rice wine)
1 tablespoon fish sauce or
    soy sauce*

For this congee, a whole duck is first cooked in a ginger infusion, then finished over rice and served with a ginger sauce. It is delicious. Ducks are also valued for their eggs, which can be preserved in salt and lime or used for desserts.

PREPARATION   *10 minutes*

✦ Wash the rice under cold running water until the water runs clear. Drain well.

COOKING   *1¼ hours*

✦ Place the duck in a large stockpot and add enough cold water to cover. Bring to a boil over medium-high heat and remove any surface fat and scum with a spoon. Add the ginger and salt, cover, reduce the heat and simmer until the duck is tender when tested in the thickest part with a fork, about 50 to 60 minutes.

✦ While the duck is cooking, heat the oil in a very large, heavy-bottomed saucepan over medium heat. Add the rice and cook, stirring frequently, until the rice is opaque, about 2 minutes. Add the onion and garlic and enough boiling water to cover the rice by 2 in (5 cm). Cover and simmer over very low heat until the rice is tender, about 25 minutes.

✦ Meanwhile, prepare the ginger sauce. Place 2 teaspoons of the grated ginger in a small mortar and crush with a pestle. Place the sugar and vinegar in a small serving bowl and stir until the sugar has dissolved. Add the fish sauce, crushed ginger and the remaining grated ginger. Mix well and set aside.

✦ Remove the duck from the stockpot, reserving the liquid. Place the duck on top of the rice in the saucepan. Cover and cook over very low heat for 10 minutes. Sprinkle the sugar over the duck and cook until the sugar melts, about 5 minutes.

✦ Meanwhile, boil the reserved duck liquid over very high heat, uncovered, until it is reduced by half.

✦ Remove the duck from the rice, slice the breast meat and cut the remainder into neat serving pieces.

✦ Divide the rice among 6 serving bowls, adding 1 to 2 tablespoons of the reduced duck liquid to each. Arrange the duck slices and pieces on top. Garnish with the scallions and mint sprigs. Serve immediately with the ginger sauce.

PER SERVING
*425 calories/1780 kilojoules; 35 g protein; 15 g fat, 32% of
calories (3.9 g saturated, 8.3% of calories; 7.4 g monounsaturated,
15.7%; 3.7 g polyunsaturated, 8%); 36 g carbohydrate;
1.5 g dietary fiber; 495 mg sodium; 3.9 mg iron;
200 mg cholesterol.*

*A paddy field
in Vietnam;
ninety percent
of the world's
rice is grown in
paddy fields.*

Duck Congee

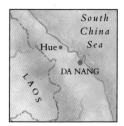

Rice Noodles with Charcoal-Grilled Pork

BUN THIT NUONG

For this easy but flavorful main dish, marinated pork is threaded on wooden skewers and cooked, then tossed with rice noodles and fragrant herbs. Nuoc cham sauce is the quintessential Vietnamese sauce.

SERVES 4

MARINADE

3 shallots (French shallots),
   chopped
3 garlic cloves, crushed
2 teaspoons sugar
½ teaspoon freshly ground black
   pepper
2 tablespoons fish sauce
1 tablespoon dry white wine
1 tablespoon vegetable oil

1 lb (500 g) pork loin (fillet),
   cut into 2 in (5 cm) cubes
8 wooden skewers
8 oz (250 g) rice noodles (rice
   vermicelli)
1 cup (2 oz/60 g) bean sprouts
¼ cup sliced scallions (spring
   onions)
¼ cup shredded mint
¼ cup shredded cilantro (coriander)
¼ cup shredded basil
1 quantity nuoc cham sauce (see
   page 54)
2 tablespoons coarsely chopped
   peanuts

PREPARATION   *30 minutes plus 4 hours marinating time*
◆ To make the marinade, place the shallots, garlic, sugar and pepper in a blender and process to a paste. Place the mixture in a large bowl. Add the fish sauce, wine and oil and combine well. Add the pork and toss gently until it is coated evenly. Cover and marinate in the refrigerator for at least 4 hours, or overnight.
◆ Soak the wooden skewers in a shallow dish of water for 30 minutes, to prevent scorching.
◆ Preheat a charcoal grill, barbecue or broiler (grill).
◆ Brush the cooking surface of the grill or barbecue with a little oil.

COOKING   *15 minutes*
◆ Thread the pork onto the bamboo skewers. Grill until browned on one side, about 2 to 3 minutes, then turn over and cook until browned and starting to crisp, about 3 minutes. Using a fork, slide the pork off the skewers onto a plate. Cover with aluminum foil to keep warm.

◆ Meanwhile, bring a large saucepan of water to a boil. Add the noodles and simmer, stirring frequently, for 3 minutes. Drain, rinse under hot running water and drain again.
◆ Place the noodles in a large, warm serving bowl. Add the pork, bean sprouts, scallions, mint, cilantro and basil. Drizzle the nuoc cham sauce on top and toss well. Then sprinkle the peanuts on top and serve immediately.

PER SERVING
494 calories/2068 kilojoules; 37 g protein; 10 g fat, 19% of calories (2.1 g saturated, 4% of calories; 3.4 g monounsaturated, 6.5%; 4.5 g polyunsaturated, 8.5%); 61 g carbohydrate; 2.1 g dietary fiber; 374 mg sodium; 3.3 mg iron; 61 mg cholesterol.

Rice Noodles with Charcoal-Grilled Pork

Chickpeas

Special Ingredients

BASIL

Basil is an annual herb with aromatic leaves that add a distinctive flavor to many dishes. It is thought to have grown first in tropical Asia and Africa and was known in ancient Egypt, Rome and Greece. There are a number of varieties of basil available today. Sweet basil is used in Mediterranean cuisine, while the main varieties used in Vietnamese (as well as Laotian and Thai) cooking are hot basil, also known as holy or heavenly basil or hairy basil, and purple basil which has the fragrance of cloves. If hairy or purple basil are not available, sweet basil may be used instead. Although dried basil is available, fresh leaves have a sweet pungent flavor and should be used when possible.

Basil

BASMATI RICE

This long-grain, fine-textured rice is grown in the foothills of the Himalayas and is the best rice to eat with Indian food. It must be washed and drained thoroughly before being cooked. Basmati rice is aged to lower its moisture content. This process helps the grains retain a firm texture when cooked as well as allowing the fragrant, nutty flavor and aroma to develop. It is available from Asian food stores and some supermarkets.

BOUQUET GARNI

A bouquet garni is a bundle of either fresh or dried herbs and/or spices used to add flavor to stocks, soups and slow-cooking dishes such as stews without the herbs dispersing throughout the liquid. The bouquet garni makes it easy to remove the herbs before serving. When fresh herbs are used, they are either tied together by their stalks with cooking twine or thread, or the herbs are wrapped up with the stalks of a flavorsome vegetable such as celery or leek. In the case of a bouquet garni made from dried herbs, their leaves are enclosed in a square of cheesecloth and secured with thread. The traditional French bouquet garni combination is parsley, bay leaves and thyme, but depending on the type of dish being cooked, other herbs, spices or vegetables can be used. They can be easily prepared at home, but the dried variety is available from specialty food stores.

BULGHUR

A staple grain of the Middle East and eastern Europe, bulghur is now widely used in Middle Eastern and Mediterranean cooking. It is used in soups, salads and cooked meat or vegetable dishes. Bulghur is whole wheat which has been steamed, dried and then cracked. It is not to be confused with cracked wheat which is uncooked. If cracked wheat is substituted for bulghur, the cooking time must be extended. Bulghur has a tender, chewy texture and can be either light or dark in color and fine, medium or coarse in granulation. It is available from health food stores, specialty food stores and some supermarkets and is sold under a variety of names, the most common being bulghur, bulgur and burghul. It should be stored in an airtight container in a cool, dark place.

CHICKPEAS

The chickpea *(Cicer arietinum)* is grown throughout the Middle East, India and southern Europe. A nutty flavored legume, the chickpea is an excellent source of carbohydrate and protein. It is considered indispensable in North African cooking and is an important part of a vegetarian diet. In India it is a popular street stall snack food, usually sold roasted and spiced or salted. Used in soups, stews, puréed and as a garnish, chickpeas are available dried, or precooked in cans. Dried chickpeas must be soaked for up to 12 hours before cooking.

CHINESE WATER CHESTNUTS

Chinese water chestnuts *(Trappa* spp) are not nuts but the corms of aquatic plants grown mainly in Southeast Asia. About the size of walnuts, their skin is similar in color to tree chestnuts. Water chestnuts feature in Asian cuisine, particularly Chinese and Vietnamese dishes. Their bland, sweetish flesh and crunchy consistency make them ideal for use in stir-fries and in stuffings. They can be coarsely chopped and combined with finely diced meat or fish to form meatballs or fishballs. Chinese water chestnuts are also ground to make a powder or flour and used as a thickening agent in a manner similar to cornstarch (cornflour). They are sold fresh from Asian or specialty food stores. Once peeled, they must be kept in water in the refrigerator and used within 3 or 4 days. Canned water chestnuts are available from most large supermarkets. Once opened, store them in water in the refrigerator in an airtight container and use them within one week.

CHORIZO

This spicy, dry sausage was first made in Spain, where it comes in many different varieties. All chorizos contain pork. Hanging in a fifteenth-century Spanish kitchen, they would attest to the owner's Christianity, serving as visual proof to the Inquisition that no one of the Jewish or Muslim faith lived there. In addition to pork, another essential ingredient of chorizo is paprika, sweet or spicy, although other minced meats and seasonings may be added as well. Spanish chorizo is made with smoked pork whereas Mexican chorizo is made with fresh. Chorizo contains very little fat and can be eaten raw, thinly sliced and served with bread, wine and olives; or it can be broiled (grilled), fried or cut in chunks and simmered in casseroles and soups.

COUSCOUS

Couscous is made from semolina, which is coarsely ground durum wheat. The grains of semolina are sprinkled with flour and water, then rubbed, either by hand or machine, into tiny pellets. Couscous was made in the deserts of North Africa for centuries by the Berber tribes, though they originally made it with millet, not wheat. Couscous may be steamed over water and served like pasta as an accompaniment to other main dishes, or it can be mixed with honey, fruit or nuts and served as a dessert. While couscous is still made by hand in North Africa, and this handmade variety can be bought from some gourmet or Middle Eastern food stores, the machine-made variety is more readily available. Packaged pre-cooked couscous is also available.

Couscous

CURRY LEAVES

The highly aromatic curry leaf comes from the curry leaf tree *(Murraya koenigii)*, an evergreen that is native to India and Sri Lanka. The tree's leaves are small, dark green and glossy, with a strong pungent aroma. Curry leaves are used in many Southwest Asian cuisines in curries and marinades. They are also used in some prepared curry mixes. In Western countries they can sometimes be purchased fresh or frozen, but are more likely to be found dried. The dried leaves are sold in many Asian food stores. If using fresh curry leaves, buy green ones with no signs of yellowing or wilting. Tear them to release the volatile oils which give them their flavor. The fresh leaves can be stored in the refrigerator in plastic wrap for several days. Fresh leaves can also be frozen. Store dried curry leaves in a tightly sealed container.

DAIKON

Daikon, also known as Japanese radish, is a giant white radish that can grow to over 2 feet (60 cm) long. It has a sweet, fresh flavor and is widely used in Asian cuisines. In Japan it is eaten raw in salads, shredded as a garnish or grated as an accompaniment to fish dishes, as well as being pickled as a relish, simmered in soups and broths or cooked as a vegetable. It is available from Asian food stores. It is best to buy white, firm small daikon as they are more tender and juicy than the larger ones. Daikon will keep in the vegetable compartment of the refrigerator for up to 2 weeks.

DRIED SHRIMP

Dried shrimp feature in many Asian cuisines, particularly in Thailand, Indonesia, Malaysia and Vietnam. They are produced by salting and then drying shrimp and are available, either whole or ground into a powder, from most specialty Asian food stores. Dried

Curry leaves

shrimp powder will lose its potency fairly quickly, so store the powder in an airtight container; it does not need refrigeration.

EDIBLE FLOWERS

Many flowers are attractive and delicious in salads and as garnishes. It is safer to buy edible flowers from specialty food stores or to pick your own from the garden. Do not use flowers that have been sprayed with pesticides and check that a particular flower is not poisonous before using it. Flowers that are commonly used include pansies, violas, nasturtiums, carnations, roses, lilacs, borage, chive flowers, marigolds and orange blossoms.

FISH SAUCE

Fish sauce is indispensable to many Southeast Asian cuisines. It is made by placing salted small fish such as anchovies, or shellfish such as shrimp, in jars or barrels and allowing them to ferment over a few months. The resulting liquid—fish sauce—is collected, strained and then bottled. The concentrated fish left after the liquid has been drawn off is used in fish dishes for a stronger flavor. Varying in color from golden to dark brown, fish sauce is known by different names in different countries; for example, *nam pla* in Thailand, and *nuoc cham* or *nuoc mam* in Vietnam, Laos and Kampuchea. Used as a condiment in a similar manner to soy sauce or anchovy essence, there is no substitute for its distinctive salty flavor. Look for fish sauce in Asian food stores. Once opened, it will keep for several months in the refrigerator.

GALANGAL

Galangal *(Alpinia galangal)* is known as *kha* in Thailand and *laos* in Indonesia. Native to Southeast Asia and China, this semitropical plant has been used for at least one thousand years. Deep buff colored and smooth skinned, galangal resembles ginger but is more delicate and fragrant in flavor. It is used extensively in Southeast Asian and Indian cooking. Galangal is sold by Asian food stores and some supermarkets. If fresh galangal is unavailable, dried or preserved galangal may be substituted. Dried galangal has to be reconstituted in hot water for one hour before using. Powdered galangal is also available.

Galangal

GHEE

Ghee has been used in Indian cooking for well over 2000 years. It is also used in other Asian cooking, although in some countries the ghee is made from the milk of the water buffalo rather than the cow. Ghee is a type of clarified butter and is ideal for sautéeing and frying. It imparts a lovely color and flavor to cooked food. It is available from specialty food stores and some supermarkets. Ghee can be frozen for up to one year or stored, tightly wrapped, in the refrigerator for up to 6 months. If butter is used in a recipe instead of ghee, it will need to be clarified. To clarify, melt the butter in a small saucepan over low heat. When the butter is simmering, continually skim the froth from the surface until only clear liquid remains, about 5 minutes.

HARISSA SAUCE

This very hot sauce is widely used in North African cooking. Its ingredients usually include dried hot chilies, olive oil, garlic, cumin, coriander and caraway seeds. Harissa sauce is traditionally used as an accompaniment to couscous, and is also used to flavor soups and casseroles. This versatile sauce is also used as a condiment and served with bread, butter and olives at the beginning of a meal. It is available in cans, jars or tubes from specialty food stores. Once opened, it can be stored in a covered glass container in the refrigerator for several weeks.

KAFFIR LIME LEAVES

The kaffir lime, called *magrut* in Thailand, has a rough, knobbly, dark green skin and is a similar size to the common lime. The leaves, the peel and the juice are widely used in Asian cuisine. Fresh leaves are not always available, but frozen or dried leaves are often sold by Asian food stores. If dried leaves are to be used, they must be soaked in water first. Lime or lemon leaves can be substituted for kaffir lime leaves, but the flavor is not as strong nor as sharp.

KASHA

Buckwheat *(Fagopyrum esculentum)* is an herb which is native to central and northern Asia. It is not a true grain, although it is nutritionally very close to grain. Kasha is the hulled, cracked kernels, or groats, of buckwheat and is used in Russian and some Middle Eastern cooking. It has a strong, nutty flavor and texture and a distinctive aroma, and is available in fine, medium or coarse grind forms from some supermarkets or health food stores. Kasha is usually cooked in a similar way to rice and can be combined with vegetables to make a vegetarian meal or served as a side dish with meatballs and broiled (grilled) fish.

KOMBU

This variety of dried Japanese seaweed is an essential ingredient of dashi, the quintessential Japanese fish stock. Also known as konbu, kombu is greenish black in color and sun-dried. It is sold in strips by Asian food stores. Before use, it should be lightly wiped to remove any powdery salt deposits, and then scored to help release its characteristic sea flavor. After cooking, kombu can be retrieved from the stock, wiped clean and stored in an airtight container in a dry, cool place for reuse. However, its flavor will decrease with subsequent use. Kombu can also be cooked as a vegetable, or pickled as a relish.

LEMONGRASS

Also known as citronella, lemongrass is an aromatic herb that grows in most tropical countries. The lower, more tender part of the stem is pounded to release its strong lemon flavor. This is then added to a dish to give it the sharp freshness that is so characteristic of Thai and other Asian cuisines. Its bulbous base is cut up and used in curries. Lemongrass can be bought in jars, dried or in powdered form, but the flavor is not as intense as the fresh lemongrass stalks which are readily available from Asian food stores. The fresh stalks should be kept in the refrigerator.

Okra

LENTILS AND OTHER PULSES

Pulses are the dried seeds of legumes, of which there are hundreds of species. Some of the most popular pulses include soybeans, dried split peas and beans, urad dal and chana dal from India and lentils. Lentils, for example, vary in color from green to brown to bright orange. They have been cultivated since ancient times in places as far apart as Switzerland and China. An excellent source of vegetable protein and some of the B vitamins, pulses have long been a staple part of the diet of people with limited access to meat and fish and are also popular with vegetarians. Pulses are most frequently used in soups and stews and of course in dal from India. Most pulses are readily available though some, such as chana dal and urad dal, may have to be purchased from specialty food stores. Stored in a cool, dark place, pulses will keep indefinitely.

Red lentils

NORI

In Japan, this type of seaweed is used dried to wrap sushi, or crushed and used as a garnish over soups, noodles and rice. The delicate flavor carries a hint of the ocean. It is also a widely used ingredient in Korean cuisine where it is known as *keem*. Nori is sold in paper-thin strips, in colors ranging from deep green to deep purple to black, and is best lightly toasted before use. Available from Asian food stores or health food shops, nori must be kept completely dry to prevent mildew from developing. It is also available toasted, and then it is known as *yakinori*.

OKRA

Okra is the green pod or fruit of the herb *Abelmoschus esculentus*. It is one of the essential ingredients of Greek, Middle Eastern, Cajun, Caribbean and South American cooking. Okra is also known as ladies' fingers, bamia and gumbo. It is best used when very young, before the seeds are completely formed. The pods, cooked whole or sliced, impart a distinctive flavor as well as a gelatinous texture, which makes them an excellent addition to soups and casseroles. They can also be steamed, sautéed, braised, used in salads or as an accompaniment to rice or meat dishes.

PALM SUGAR

Palm sugar is processed from the sap of the palmyra palm *(Borassus flabellifer),* which is native to much of Southeast Asia. Records show that it was used in China almost 2000 years ago. It is used throughout Asia, and is known as n*am taan peep* in Thailand, *gula Java* in Indonesia, *jaggery* in India, Burma and Sri Lanka, and *gula Malacca* in Malaysia. The strong flavor of palm sugar gives richness to both sweet and savory dishes. It is sold compressed into round or rectangular shapes (which may need to be grated before use), or in round slightly domed cakes, or as a thick paste. If it is unavailable, substitute soft brown sugar or demerara sugar. Stored in cool, dry conditions, palm sugar keeps for several years.

PARMESAN

Parmesan *(parmigiano)* is one of the most famous Italian cheeses. It is ideal for cooking and melts easily while retaining its distinctive, piquant flavor. This hard, dry cheese is grated over pasta dishes, eaten freshly cut with fruit, and also complements soups, sauces and soufflés. If well-wrapped, solid Parmesan can be kept almost indefinitely in the refrigerator. Factory-grated Parmesan can be found in most supermarkets, but the flavor is not as good as that of freshly grated Parmesan, which can be bought from delicatessens and specialty food stores.

PARSLEY

Parsley is a biennial plant that has been widely used for centuries. Today parsley is one of the most widely grown and used herbs. Rich in vitamins A, B and especially C, parsley enhances other flavors and is one of the main components of a bouquet garni. It complements just about every savory dish and makes an attractive and delicious garnish. It is also used in marinades, stocks, soups, sauces and vinaigrettes, and can be added to butter to make a delicious spread. The most popular varieties of parsley are the curly-leaf and flat-leaf (or Italian) types. Curly-leaf parsley is excellent for garnishing and salads while the stronger flavored flat-leaf parsley is good for cooking. Parsley can easily be grown in a garden or in a pot on a sunny window sill. Fresh parsley is best stored in the refrigerator with its stems in water or wrapped in plastic and stored in the crisper.

Parsley

Saffron

PHYLLO PASTRY

These paper-thin sheets of pastry are widely used in Greek and Middle Eastern cooking and are sometimes spelled filo or fillo. Made with a high-gluten flour and little fat, the pastry is very pliable and so is ideal for wrapping ingredients into small, individual food parcels. It is also used for traditional pies. Phyllo pastry is used to make both savory and sweet dishes. It is difficult to make, but it can be purchased chilled or frozen from most supermarkets.

POMEGRANATES

The pomegranate *(Punica granatum)* is native to the Mediterranean area and southern Asia but now it is grown in many tropical and subtropical regions. Mentioned in the Bible and in stories of Mohammed, the fruit has a thin but hard skin, generally a pink orange color. The sweet-tart seeds and pulp are enjoyed on their own and are also used as a garnish, because of their beautiful appearance. The seeds can be boiled down to produce a syrup which, unsweetened, is used in savory dishes, particularly in the Middle East. The juice of the pomegranate is also made into grenadine, a sweet syrup which adds color and flavor to desserts and drinks. Choose fruit that have a heavy feel to them, and a shiny skin. Store in the refrigerator for up to 2 months.

Pomegranates

RICE VINEGAR

Rice vinegar is made in an age-old traditional process from fermented rice and is a feature of a number of Asian cuisines, particularly those of Japan and China. Japanese rice vinegar, which is known as *su,* has a mild sweetish flavor and is an essential component of sushi. Chinese rice vinegars are available in three main types: clear, which is the most commonly used; red, which features in sauces and dips; and black, which has a stronger flavor with a slight sweetness and is often used as a condiment. The vinegars can vary in flavor and strength according to their place of origin. As with other styles of vinegars, the more expensive brands tend to be of a superior quality. Store in the refrigerator. Rice vinegars are available from large supermarkets and Asian specialty stores. A mild white wine or cider vinegar can be substituted if rice vinegar is unobtainable.

RICE WINE

The taste and golden color of Chinese rice wine *(shao hsing)* is reminiscent of malt whiskey. The preparation and making of rice wine in China has been recorded since the time of Confucius. A vital ingredient in many Chinese dishes, rice wine is also used as a marinade and is added to stir-fry recipes. Chinese rice wine is also drunk warm as an accompaniment to meals. Stored in a cool, dark place, it will keep for a long period of time, but its flavor will lessen with age.

SAFFRON

Saffron is made from the dried stigmas of the autumn-flowering crocus *(Crocus sativus).* The flowers have to be picked by hand and as about 150,000 flowers are needed to obtain 2 pounds (1 kilogram) of saffron, it is clearly the most expensive spice in the world. The plant originated in Asia Minor and was later taken to the Mediterranean region and now Spain is the world's major producer. Saffron has always been used in cooking, but in ancient times it was also extensively used for medicinal purposes and as a clothing dye. However, it is now too expensive for this, although in India it may still be used to dye the veil of a bride. Saffron is intensely aromatic, with a slightly pungent flavor, and gives a beautiful yellow color to any dish to which it is added. It is available in powdered form, as well, though the powder is considered inferior to the threads. It should be stored in an airtight container.

SAMBAL ULEK (SAMBAL BAJAK)

This Indonesian chili sauce is widely used in Indonesia, Malaysia and southern India as a seasoning and served with a variety of curries and rice dishes as either a condiment or a side dish. It is usually made from a base of chilies ground in a stone pestle called a ulekan. Sambal ulek is available in glass jars from specialty food stores and can be kept in the refrigerator for several months.

SANSHO PEPPER

Sansho pepper is in fact a Japanese spice which is usually sprinkled on chicken dishes, noodles and soups, giving them a mildly hot and citrus flavor. The leaves of the prickly ash tree *(Zanthoxylum piperitum)* are dried and ground to make the greenish brown spice which is also used in the Japanese seven-spice blend known as *shichimi.* Sansho pepper can be bought from Asian food stores and should be stored in an airtight container. It is best to buy sansho in small quantities as it loses its flavor quickly.

SHALLOTS (FRENCH SHALLOTS)

The shallot is similar in taste to both onion and garlic. Somewhat larger than garlic, it also forms a bulb, but its tough outer skin is deep golden brown in color. Greatly favored in traditional French cuisine, the shallot also features prominently in the cooking of China,

Shallots

Vietnam and the Indian subcontinent. It is particularly useful for flavoring sauces because the shallot will emulsify more easily than the onion. It is a good choice for salads and as a complement to lighter flavored foods such as fish and chicken. Keep shallots in a well-ventilated place, but not in the refrigerator as other foods may absorb their flavor. Be sure when buying them that they are plump and firm.

SOBA NOODLES

Soba noodles are made from buckwheat (a nutritious, gluten-free cereal grass) and ordinary wheat mixed together. The long thin noodles are light beige in color. However, there are variations such as the popular *cha-soba* where green tea *(cha)* is added to the dough, giving color and extra flavor. The popularity of soba noodles is immense in Japan where there are over 50,000 soba restaurants. In these restaurants, the quiet and peaceful atmosphere that usually accompanies Japanese meals is replaced by the customary loud "slurping" of the soba noodles. Another tradition in Japan concerning soba noodles

Soba noodles

is that they are the last dish eaten on New Year's Eve. Most Asian food stores in the West sell these noodles only in their dried form.

SOYBEAN PASTE

Soybeans have played an important part in the diets of the peoples of Asia. After being fermented, the beans are processed into a variety of sauces and pastes which are used to add flavor and color. Soybean paste (also marketed as soybean sauce) has a strong, salty flavor and can be either smooth in texture or still contain whole beans within the paste. The paste is used where a thicker sauce is required than would be provided by the more usual soy sauce. It is available in jars or cans from specialty Asian food stores, and once opened, should be refrigerated.

TOFU

Tofu is a product of soybean milk that is curdled to produce an easily digested and nutritious "cheese." Tofu, also known as beancurd, originated in China about 2000 years ago and was later taken to Japan by Buddhist monks. An important and inexpensive source of protein in Asian cooking, it is used in a multitude of ways: stuffed, diced, shredded and puréed. Because of its protein content, tofu is also valued by vegetarians. Available in Asian food stores, most health food shops and some general supermarkets, it is usually sold in blocks surrounded by liquid. It is also sometimes available in powdered form.

WASABI

Wasabi is made from the root of *Wasabia japonica,* a plant native to Japan and similar to the horseradish root. Hence, wasabi is sometimes known as Japanese horseradish.

The root has a brown skin and pale green flesh and its flavor is more fragrant and less pungent than horseradish. Hotter than even the hottest chilies, wasabi is served sparingly as a condiment with a number of Japanese dishes. The Japanese pickle, *wasabi-zuke,* is made by pickling wasabi in sake. To prepare fresh wasabi for use as a condiment, peel and grate the root. Although the fresh root is not readily available in Western countries, wasabi is usually available in both paste (in tubes) and powdered forms from Asian grocery stores. Mix powdered wasabi with a little cold water and leave for about 10 minutes before using to allow the flavor to develop; it should not be made further in advance or it will lose its heat. Store wasabi paste in the refrigerator once opened. The powder should be stored in a container with a tight-fitting lid in a cool, dry place.

Wasabi

ZEST

The colored thin outermost peel of oranges, lemons and other citrus fruit is called zest. It contains fragrant oils and has a strong flavor. To obtain the zest, use a potato peeler, a very sharp knife, a grater or a special zester to separate it from the pith (the bitter white part of the skin). If using a peeler or a knife, cut the zest into julienne strips; if using a grater or zester, do so over the dish you are preparing to capture the oil spray. Zest is used as a flavoring in both sweet and savory dishes and also as a garnish. The most commonly used fruits for zest are oranges and lemons.

Index